Legacies of Losing
in American Politics

CHICAGO STUDIES IN AMERICAN POLITICS

A series edited by Benjamin I. Page, Susan Herbst,
Lawrence R. Jacobs, and Adam J. Berinsky

ALSO IN THE SERIES:

Additional series titles follow index

Legacies of Losing in American Politics

JEFFREY K. TULIS
NICOLE MELLOW

The University of Chicago Press ❁ Chicago and London

JEFFREY K. TULIS
teaches American politics
and political theory at
the University of Texas at
Austin and is the author
of several books, including
The Rhetorical Presidency.
NICOLE MELLOW
is professor of political
science at Williams College and the author of
The State of Disunion.

The University of Chicago Press, Chicago 60637
The University of Chicago Press, Ltd., London
© 2018 by The University of Chicago
All rights reserved. No part of this book may be used or
reproduced in any manner whatsoever without written
permission, except in the case of brief quotations in critical articles and reviews. For more information, contact
the University of Chicago Press, 1427 East 60th Street,
Chicago, IL 60637.
Published 2018
Printed in the United States of America

27 26 25 24 23 22 21 20 19 18   1 2 3 4 5

ISBN-13: 978-0-226-51529-8 (cloth)
ISBN-13: 978-0-226-51532-8 (paper)
ISBN-13: 978-0-226-51546-5 (e-book)
DOI: 10.7208/chicago/9780226515465.001.0001

Library of Congress Cataloging-in-Publication Data

Names: Tulis, Jeffrey, author. | Mellow, Nicole, author.
Title: Legacies of losing in American politics / Jeffrey K.
Tulis, Nicole Mellow.
Other titles: Chicago studies in American politics.
Description: Chicago ; London : The University of Chicago Press, 2018. | Series: Chicago studies in American
politics | Includes bibliographical references and index.
Identifiers: LCCN 2017031817 | ISBN 9780226515298
(cloth : alk. paper) | ISBN 9780226515328
(pbk. : alk. paper) | ISBN 9780226515465 (e-book)
Subjects: LCSH: United States—Politics and government.
| Federal government—United States. | Johnson,
Andrew, 1808–1875. | Reconstruction (U.S. history,
1865–1877) | Goldwater, Barry M. (Barry Morris),
1909–1998.
Classification: LCC JK31 .T85 2018 E183 | DDC 973—dc23
LC record available at https://lccn.loc.gov/2017031817

To Walter Dean Burnham
and
To the memory of Herbert J. Storing

Contents

1

Political Failure, and Success

American politics is typically a story of winners: victorious politicians, successful social movements, effective and long-lasting political coalitions. It is not surprising that political victory is thought requisite to a genuine and lasting political legacy because, in general, that is the normal course of affairs everywhere. Founders who triumph; generals who are victorious in wars; presidents who win critical elections; social activists whose movements prevail in legislatures, in courts, and in civil society—all mark the major developmental moments in political life.

Losers in American politics tend to recede and be forgotten: Alf Landon, Henry Wallace, Wendell Willkie, Alton B. Parker, James Cox, John Anderson, Robert Dole, Michael Dukakis. Much further back in time: Charles Pinckney, Rufus King, Lewis Cass, Winfield Scott, John C. Breckinridge, Horatio Seymour. They were all presidential candidates. Few remember their names, and those who do care little about them. For political stability and legitimacy, the fading away of losers may be a helpful feature of American politics. At the presidential level, American candidates have almost always been good losers, in the idiom of sportsmanship. For example, the presidential election of 2000 was the closest election in American history. Ballots were challenged in Florida, and the outcome of the election was delayed until the Supreme Court ruled that there was insufficient time and insufficient legal justification for a recount. Almost immediately upon learning of the court's decision, the losing candidate, Albert Gore, conceded to George W. Bush. After an exchange of speeches, a frenzied election was over and a peaceful transition of power ensued. Though the incidents are often less dramatic, American history is replete with examples of losers who conceded gracefully and disappeared into the background.[1]

Nested within this congenial picture of legitimacy and stability, however, is also one of disruption and challenge. Some losers do not fade away but, instead, live on and reshape the political landscape. *Legacies of Losing in American Politics* is an account of three such losers, and the chronicle that emerges forces us to rethink conventional narratives of American politics. In three separate and pivotal developmental moments of American political history, prominent political actors were vanquished decisively; yet these losers eventually achieved success for their ideas and preferred policies. At the Founding, the Anti-Federalists failed in their effort to defeat ratification of the Constitution. In the immediate aftermath of the Civil War, President Andrew Johnson's plan for restoring the South to the Union was defeated by Radical Republicans, who instead imposed Reconstruction. And in the 1964 presidential campaign, Barry Goldwater's robust challenge to the New Deal order was soundly defeated by President Lyndon Johnson. The irrefutable nature of these three losses at the time they occurred served to underscore the significance of the success of their opposition. The Founding, Reconstruction (often called "the second founding"), and the New Deal are typically heralded as the most significant turning points in the country's history, with many observers seeing each of these as political triumphs through which the United States has come to more closely realize its liberal ideals of liberty and equality. Yet our study of the losers in these moments shows that rather than disappearing under the currents of liberal progress, the Anti-Federalists, Andrew Johnson, and Barry Goldwater facilitated future successes for their defeated political programs. Understanding the legacies of these three losses in American politics is our principal aim.

By focusing on what we call the "antimoments" to the well-known political victories of the Founding, Reconstruction, and New Deal, *Legacies of Losing in American Politics* offers a new way of thinking about American political development. The initial policy and ideational defeats represented in these antimoments later transformed themselves into long-term successes. Our main goals are to describe the substantive agenda sought by the key actors in each case, to reveal the mechanisms by which the early failures facilitated long-term successes, and to show that fresh thinking about these hitherto neglected phenomena provides fertile ground to modify, if not recast, two major synoptic perspectives on American politics. Taken together, these particular cases offer a new window on American politics as a whole.

Synoptic Perspectives

Among students of American political development, two narratives of American politics loom especially large. One focuses on the idea that there are moments of profound regime-level *change* in American politics that usher in fundamentally new political orders. The other narrative focuses on *continuities* in American political life, beginning with the assertion of the hegemony of liberalism, or a distinctively American creed in the constitutional order. Both narratives have generated substantial scholarly debate, and this book aims to usefully conjoin and revise these two important intellectual traditions.

For leading students of transformative change, American political history has been marked by several unusually significant moments, or breaks, when the polity has been founded or refounded. Some of the most impressive accounts of the historical trajectory of American politics—for example, books by Bruce Ackerman, Theodore Lowi, and Walter Dean Burnham—show the vital importance of transformative eras in American politics.[2] Ackerman calls these "constitutional moments." Lowi calls them

America's successive "republics." Burnham made famous the notions of "critical elections," "critical realignments," and "punctuated equilibria" and has linked these to Ackerman's account of American political development. These formative thinkers and others like them agree on the unusual times in which American politics transformed, when one era of normal politics dramatically gave way to a new and different era of normal politics. In these moments, a domestic or foreign crisis, political agitation, societal cleavages, and competing ideas and programs of action disrupted the political convention; after the dust settled, a new "normal," with new governing ideas, newly dominant interests and leaders, and new institutions came to prevail. Scholars of these sorts of transformations mark three "moments" in particular—the Founding and the ratification of the Constitution, Reconstruction after the Civil War, and the New Deal political order initiated by Franklin D. Roosevelt—as the most consequential. They are therefore of most interest to us.

It is now conventional wisdom to point to the victors in each of these three transformational occasions—the Federalists (or, more popularly, "the Founders"), Lincoln and the Republican Party, and Franklin D. Roosevelt and the New Deal Democratic Party, as the actors who decisively shaped American politics thereafter. Indeed, George Washington, Abraham Lincoln, and Franklin D. Roosevelt regularly top historians' lists of great presidents, presidents who made a profound mark on the trajectory of the country's development. The conventional wisdom also happens to be true. Politics before and after each moment was unmistakably different in terms of the dominant ideas, influential actors and interests, institutional configurations, and policy enactments. Prior to ratification of the Constitution, only a loose confederation of newly independent states existed while after came a constitutional republic on a scale not previously realized for republics. Slave states coexisted uneasily with free states and in tension with the new national government until the Civil War and Reconstruction abolished slavery and fortified the supremacy of the national government. National power was nonetheless still limited, and ideas of laissez-faire capitalism reigned until the New Deal ushered in federal government regulatory and social welfare activism and built the modern administrative state. The significance of the changes that occurred in each of these three moments is incontrovertible, and the leaders whose victories are associated with them shaped all subsequent American politics.

Yet we mean to show how it is also the case that the losers in each of these major, order-determining contests decisively shaped the subsequent course of American politics. Each constitutional moment had its antimoment, and both fundamentally shaped politics thereafter. The Anti-Federalists, Andrew Johnson, and Barry Goldwater were all regarded by their contemporaries as the losers in the immediate contests in which they engaged. In the moment, there was no question about the fact of their loss or its significance for the politics at the time: there would be a new constitution; an agenda of reconstruction, not restoration, of the postwar South would proceed; and New Deal liberalism would remain the dominant political mode, its reach expanded. When aspects or features of a politics at odds with these outcomes subsequently became visible—a forceful resurgence of states' rights after ratification of the Constitution, the emergence of Jim Crow after Reconstruction, or the success of "Reagan Republicanism," for example—observers have typically misapprehended the significance and failed to recognize the earlier antimoment losers as sources of these seemingly anachronistic political developments.

These antimoments, while sometimes individually recognized, have yet to be sufficiently theorized or even studied as part of a larger phenomenon of American political development. Occasionally, one of these losers, in isolation, has been retrospectively identified as a herald of future political developments, even while their influence on that development is underappreciated. Not only do we uncover the ways in which the failure of each of our losers helped to facilitate the eventual success of the losers' programs, but we also bring these episodes together to generate a new account of transformational change. More precisely, our cases are especially interesting because they supplement and complicate the well-known studies of transformation. Although we show that the constitutional moments that concern scholars were not as unequivocally transformative as has been claimed, the fact that our losers eventually won does not mean that the well-known winners eventually lost. The cases don't "refute" Ackerman, Lowi, Burnham, and others. Rather, our cases make more complex the story of winning and losing that is traditionally told. If we are correct in our assessment of these self-transforming defeats, then much of the current understanding of the character of the American constitutional order, and the logic of its change—advanced or presumed by the "constitutional moments" perspective—needs to be modified. Rather than a narrative of liberal constitutional progress, we offer an interpretation of a braided developmental process in which liberal constitutional moments are entwined with constitutional antimoments that sustain and ingrain illiberalisms or ascriptive hierarchies.

The other synoptic perspective that interests us, and one from which the constitutional moments conversation was born, is the even more fundamental claim that America has a hegemonic liberal tradition that marks it as distinct from other advanced industrial democracies. The claims about the foundational nature of American liberalism, American exceptionalism, or the American creed are well known, and we need not belabor them here. From Tocqueville's assessment of a nation "born equal" to Hartz's assertion that a country lacking a feudal past had no socialist future, the view that the United States is indefatigably liberal—committed to the political ideals of individual liberty, equality, and the rule of law—is one of the most influential ideas in the study of American politics.[3] Even those who resist the claim that there is no real conflict in America because of the liberal consensus nonetheless often subscribe to the liberal narrative as America's aspirational or regulative ideal. In addition to the work of scholars, such as Samuel Huntington, who see conflict in American political history as a regularized effort to better realize liberal ideals, the story of America's constitutional moments, outlined above, is inscribed with a narrative of liberal progress.[4]

So profound is the claim about American liberalism that most scholarship in American political science simply assumes this feature of the political order, even if the research effort undertaken is to explain time- and place-based departures from it. In recent years, however, the liberal tradition thesis has become the subject of much of the most interesting work in political science about American politics, work that seeks to better understand the nature of the polity and the deep sources of political conflict and change. In this genre, Rogers Smith's "multiple traditions" thesis is seminal. In his pathbreaking work, Smith shows that alongside the American liberal tradition are persistent republican and "ascriptive" traditions that have been overlooked by scholars. These other traditions are of sufficient duration and consequence to require, in Smith's view, a redefinition of American political identity and culture beyond liberalism alone.[5] Other scholars have elaborated the challenge to the theory of American liberalism by identifying other political traditions, such as a persistent moralism, or by seeking to explain evidence of citizenship hierarchies despite the country's de jure liberal commitments.[6]

Because the ascriptive tradition, which defends inequality and hierarchy, runs so counter to the dominant American liberal creed, how it has been sustained remains something of a puzzle and, of course, given the attention to racial and other animosities at the current moment, an especially aggravating puzzle. Our book begins to provide an answer. The ascriptive tradition is not just a bottom-up phenomenon sustained by fringe groups, state and local laws, and the customs and prejudices of once-powerful majorities. As our cases show, this tradition is also an inheritance sustained and facilitated by the actions of leaders at the national level. Because the cases of antimoments we examine here have not previously been studied together, nor has the significance of the failure-to-success leadership phenomenon we identify been previously revealed, our choice of cases allows us to show how the narrative of progressive liberal transformations across American history is only part of the story. We show that another part of the story of America is a regressive tradition of citizenship hierarchies that flourishes anew each time it is believed to have been vanquished, and that the currents of one antimoment loss feed and inform the subsequent moments. This is at the heart of our concept of braided constitutional development.

Offering correctives to these two synoptic views of American politics is the ultimate payoff of the three cases that form the core of our book, and we will return to them at greater length in chapter 5. Although we mean to intervene in these two debates and offer our own big picture of the character of American politics, the bulk of our book is devoted to depicting the three cases in sufficient detail that the many scholars engaged in these debates will have to take our three cases into account whether or not they agree with our interpretations of their significance.

The Three Antimoments

As should be clear by this point, our cases—those of the Anti-Federalists, Andrew Johnson, and Barry Goldwater—were chosen as occasions to rethink the significance of the most crucial junctures in American politics, those of the Founding, Reconstruction, and the New Deal. Extraordinary moments in political time govern our choice of these extraordinary cases. In each instance, we sought to identify the most robust challenge to the "constitutional moment" at hand. In the case of the Founding, it was the ratification battle and thus our focus is on the Anti-Federalists who waged that battle. As we explain in chapter 2 and as is well known by scholars of this era's politics, ratification was by no means assured, and the rhetorical and strategic assault launched by the Anti-Federalists was formidable. That they were defeated makes the triumph of the Federalists' constitution all the more profound, but our goal in this chapter is to show how the Anti-Federalist loss was nonetheless reconfigured into a powerfully lasting legacy for American politics.

The possibilities during the era of Reconstruction were, in a sense, without precedent in this country because of the uniqueness of the victory in civil war; it was a moment for the victorious North, with its total control of national government and military power, to redefine the terms of the still young Union. Andrew Johnson stood in the way, and his loss is thus celebrated as evidence of the nation's forward march toward greater equality and liberty. Yet we show in chapter 3 how Johnson ultimately took advantage of the postwar disarray, drawing rhetorical resources from the Anti-Federalist legacy and supplying new strategies to ultimately thwart and undermine the Reconstruction agenda imposed against his will during his presidency. The Jim Crow challenge to the Reconstruction agenda cannot be understood without first grappling with Johnson's legacy for the South and the nation.

Finally, we chose Barry Goldwater as the antimoment to the New Deal because the Democratic order was flourishing in the early 1960s, finding new articulation in the presidencies of John Kennedy and then Lyndon Johnson. Unlike other earlier, successful Republicans of the era (Dwight Eisenhower, Nelson Rockefeller, or even Richard Nixon, for example), Goldwater's candidacy represented the first real and significant challenge to the New Deal order, one that struck at the heart of its presumptions and its ideological claims. That the American electorate so soundly rebuffed Goldwater was taken to be evidence of the continued power of New Deal Democratic ideas. Chapter 4 shows how every dimension of his loss helped bring about Ronald Reagan's and modern conservatism's eventual success. Because Goldwater's campaign supporters trafficked, sometimes recklessly, in the legacies of the earlier losses we describe—those of the Anti-Federalists and of Johnson—the subsequent success of modern conservatism brought with it features Goldwater endorsed as well as those that he, himself, would repudiate.

Beyond their significance as antimoments, our cases are interesting and useful for additional reasons. First, they invite consideration of the relationship between loss and success in very different contexts: constitution making, legislative and policy leadership, and presidential election campaigning. Each of the three cases has a different central actor: a social movement, a president, and a candidate, respectively. How victory was sought—and initially denied—is also different in each case: an antiratification contest waged, and lost, in state conventions and newspaper editorials; a postwar reunification battle waged between a president and Congress, with the former's terms of settlement defeated and he politically routed; and a presidential electoral contest in which the challenger was decisively trounced. In all the cases, however, the central actors sought to persuade others of the superiority of their ideas and to promote related laws and policies. And in all three cases, these desired and significant ideas and policy outcomes were, after being initially decisively defeated, subsequently realized. That success was achieved in each, and yet that the relationship of loss to success occurred in such different contexts, is to us provocative and fascinating. And we believe the fact that the relationship transcends the particulars of each case attests to the power of the antimoment current in American politics.

If we are successful in prosecuting our argument about antimoment losses and their legacies, this may prompt inquiry into the large array of topics opened up by our new way of thinking about political loss. Others may seek to develop a general theory of the conditions under which losing is likely to lead to success in the long run. We do not do that here. Our cases were not chosen with that kind of project in mind—though we would be delighted if others are prompted to attempt it. But before one could select a sample of cases designed to test hypotheses regarding conditions for a "successful loss," one would first need to understand what it means to lose successfully. Our cases are well suited for establishing this conceptual foundation. More importantly, for our principal aim—to reinterpret the significance of constitutional moments in American political development— our three core chapters do not represent a sample but, rather, are the entire set of relevant cases.

Rethinking the Vocabulary of Politics

Our argument is that in each of our cases, failure facilitated eventual success. These are failures that did not merely anticipate, nor merely preview, a future but were rather modes of agency that helped to bring about success. Because we know of no work that explores the idea of self-transforming failure as we do, we also offer this book as an opening or invitation to expand the general scholarly agenda of political science. This subsidiary aim of this book grew out of our effort to comprehend the significance of the constitutional antimoments on which we focus.

We make two unconventional arguments in this regard. First, we suggest that, in the long run, it might *sometimes* be better to lose than to win an electoral or legislative contest as it initially unfolds. In some circumstances, winning can actually be a kind of loss and, conversely, losing can be a kind of win. If one absorbs the lessons of the cases we present, then one must contend seriously with this more general conclusion. Second, we suggest that the particular mechanisms by which a political contest is lost may sometimes become the very means to transform that loss or failure into a win or success in the long term. This too, we believe, is illustrated by our cases, and thus, we offer the general observation that in some circumstances mechanisms of loss may themselves be agents of change. Because these counterintuitive processes may be of interest to students of other aspects of American or comparative politics, we conclude this chapter with reflections on political *reversal* (loss may be success and success may be loss under some conditions) and on political *agency* (mechanisms of initial loss may become mechanisms for success in the long run). We elaborate these notions for students of politics generally by showing how they frame our account of America's three great constitutional transformations specifically.

REVERSAL

In the course of our investigation, it was necessary to rethink basic terms of political vocabulary—terms such as "loss," "defeat," "success," and "victory." It is difficult to make sense of the political trajectories we trace using the conventional terms ascribed to the actors and actions we document. For example, conservatives today hail Barry Goldwater as a hero. Many of his policy aims are ones they now claim in their own efforts to get elected and implement once elected. Yet Goldwater's landslide loss in 1964 is indisputable and, at the time, few outside of his most devoted followers would have predicted that in just one or two political generations his ideas would have mainstream support. To speak of Goldwater's defeat in 1964 in conventional form—as a loss—misses the fact that features of this loss generated the conditions for the eventual success and popularity of many of his aims. Do we think of Goldwater as a loser because of the 1964 contest or a winner because of the achievement of his goals through means initiated by that 1964 loss? Should winning office by abandoning the ends for which one seeks power be thought a victory, while achieving those ends by electoral defeat be thought a loss? Our account thus invites a reconsideration of conventional conceptions. In this book, we demonstrate that indisputable political losses can, in fact, yield significant and lasting victory for ideas presumed to have been defeated. American political development cannot be understood without an account of these kinds of losers: movements, coalitions, candidates, and officeholders whose defeated political visions prevail over time.

Very few scholars have noticed the long-term success of stunning political defeats, let alone studied their dynamics. Rather than being conceived as an alternative kind of success, loss, when it is studied, is almost always treated as an aspect of the familiar narratives of victory. Scholars show the mistakes that resulted in the loss, the conditions that prevented success, or the policy and developmental paths that were foreclosed by the loss.[7] In conventional accounts of American politics, failure can illustrate the lasting power of political victories and the conditions and strategies behind them by contrast with paths not taken or influences not felt. But political success is the premise in all of these, and it is the empirical and normative benchmark against which loss is measured. Success, conventionally defined, remains the lens through which political loss is examined, and better understanding conventional electoral and legislative success remains the purpose of studying loss.

Other, perhaps less conventional, accounts of failure show the limitations of campaigns generally understood to be successful. For example, recent work by Ira Katznelson demonstrates how widely lauded New Deal and World War II benefit programs in fact exacerbated and entrenched racial economic hierarchies.[8] Mary Frances Berry describes the civil rights movement during the Reagan presidency as "winning while losing." Although the Legislative Conference on Civil Rights led a coalition of civil rights organizations and activists to significant legislative victories, they eventually lost the law and policy struggle to Reagan and his progeny. Reagan's biggest victories came through the courts.[9] And recent work on conservative retrenchment details the ways in which celebrated legal and political victories have routinely yielded less transformation than anticipated due to the Supreme Court's effort to integrate new developments with older frameworks.[10] This sort of scholarly investigation reveals failure (or falling short) to be a previously unappreciated feature of widely heralded success in American politics. The purpose of those investigations, nonetheless, is to yield new insight into conventionally recognized successes, showing that sometimes victory is not all it has been made out to be. Our theme of reversal mirrors this. We show that loss is not always the total failure it is thought to be. The two narratives are complementary. When one understands how loss transforms into success, one gains insight into the mechanisms by which success is limited or undone—at least in the case of constitutional moments.

It is not unusual for scholars to reexamine political eras or political leadership to show how what was thought to be failure is really success, or what was thought to be insignificant is truly important, or what was previously overlooked deserves to be given its due. The reevaluations of Calvin Coolidge, William McKinley, Harry Truman, Dwight Eisenhower, Jane Addams, and the role of blacks in the military all come readily to mind. In these sorts of cases, successful political or social action was overlooked or was mislabeled as failed in the first place. The purpose of studying these sorts of losses is often either to refine our understanding of leadership (highlighting, for example, Ike's "hidden-hand" style) or to show how a loser's actions enhanced the success of phenomena unrelated to his or her intentions (for example, losing an electoral contest nonetheless invigorated democratic participation).[11]

Our cases represent undeniable political loss—political efforts that were instances of genuine failure, appropriately so labeled because the facts of electoral or legislative loss in the moment remain incontestable. In the retrospective gaze of history, no one denies that the political efforts that interest us—the Anti-Federalists' effort to prevent ratification of the Constitution, Andrew Johnson's agenda for restoration of the South, and Barry Goldwater's 1964 campaign for the presidency—resulted in defeat in the moment of the contest. What we aim to uncover is how these short-term losses, more than simply opening up opportunities, helped to configure the later success of the very same ideas and policies the loser advanced. To be clear, we are not contesting that some outcomes, or paths, were denied or foreclosed for the loser in the short run. Indeed, the immediate loss itself is part of what we show facilitating eventual success. Nor are we attempting to recast total loss as partial loss because of the incremental contribution made to some larger cause. Our claim is that, in these interesting cases, total and profound loss was a constitutive feature of eventual success, and we aim to understand how the features of that loss inform, shape, and enable a successful future, as viewed from the perspective of the loser turned eventual winner. Our broader aim, as stated above, is to uncover the implications of these sorts of contests for the currents of American politics more generally. What do these particular kinds of losses do to the polity from the point of view of the constitutional order as a whole?

The conception of loss we portray is similar to one described by Deborah Stone in her classic text on policy analysis. Stone describes the Republican effort to pass a balanced budget amendment in 1995, having promised to do so in the campaign that led to their landslide midterm victory the year before. A bill successfully passed the House, but Majority Leader Robert Dole could not muster the veto-proof sixty-seven votes necessary to pass it in the Senate. Knowing he did not have the votes, Dole scheduled a vote anyway. "We really win if we win, but we may also win if we lose," he said.[12] As Stone explains, "Although a loss for the Republicans' policy goal, Dole thought it might be a gain for Republicans' political strength."[13] The vote could highlight and clarify the ideological differences between the parties and lay the groundwork for a Republican victory in the next major election. Although Republicans did gain two seats in the Senate in 1996, they failed to take the presidency. Dole's strategy does bear some resemblance to the losses we describe. However, his loss was not total or profound and his strategy was not ultimately successful. Dole was unable to translate his loss into a substantial victory for his party.

What might be gained from a consideration of reversals and from a closer inspection of such common terms of politics as "win," "loss," "victory," "defeat," "success," and "failure"? The work of other scholars on political loss cited above made us more thoughtful about our claims with regard to what might have once been seen as unquestioned political outcomes. Our focus on reversals underscores this, but we hope it does more. One of the implications of our study is that winning might not always be preferable to losing. It may be the case that there are times when being defeated advances the loser's objectives more than if she had actually "won." This way of thinking is anathema to an American culture that seems to revere winning above all else. Yet if we are right, then those who analyze politics must pay closer attention to whom or what they are tossing into the dustbin of history and what they believe has been accomplished with victory, because face-value assessments can be very wrong.

A note of caution about our ambitions is necessary here. As

stated earlier, we are not seeking to generate a general theory of when a loss becomes a success. We chose our cases because of their relationship to the key constitutional moments that other scholars have identified as critical to understanding American political history. Nonetheless, because our cases have forced us to think anew about the conventional terms of win and loss, we would be delighted if others were inspired by our insights to generate and test hypotheses about when a loss becomes a win. This might require that scholars use their own specifications of the terms we deploy here if their project is a theory of conditions under which reversal occurs. For example, we do not specify, a priori, a time by which the loss that interests us is reversed or can be called a success. The time periods for achievement of policy goals and ideational success vary in our cases. This is not surprising, as will be shown in subsequent chapters, given that the transformative context (the constitutional moment), the nature of the defeat, and the process of reversal from failure to success vary in each. For our purposes, it is not important that the reversal happen in some specified time, be it a year, five years, or two decades. Rather, we are concerned with identifying how this process has happened and the implications for the currents of American politics, writ large—what does it mean and how can it be that ideas and policies rejected as part of a moment of constitutional refounding reemerge, are endorsed, and have impact, often without being fully appreciated by the polity?

Although our concern in this book is with the reversals that constitute our three antimoments, the general idea that losing might lead to long-run success first germinated, for one of us, years ago. In a casual conversation with a political operative whose candidate had just lost an election, Tulis speculated that winning may have been worse because the policy and economic circumstances were so bleak for anyone winning office at the time. Because the prospects for policy and political success were so unfavorable, losing might ultimately turn out to be advantageous as the operative's candidate now had the opportunity to establish the political narrative by which his opponent, the winner of the electoral contest and now–elected officeholder, would be judged and held accountable in the next contest. While the operative responded, "*It is ALWAYS better to win—end of story,*" for Tulis, the idea that, in certain circumstances, losing might yield eventual, and better, success seemed a promising insight. From the perspective of the political operative, it would certainly be better for his professional reputation had his candidate won. There are other, more generous reasons why winning, conventionally defined, might be "always better." In the tumult of a political contest, candidates and their teams need positive and clear marching orders. As a political maxim, "It is always better to win" will make for more focused and effective campaigns. Moreover, the future is never certain. Unfavorable political and economic circumstances may change, whereas the opportunity to hold office may never come again. Campaigns are hard work: how can that work be done effectively if one is not committed to the most basic and obvious point of a contest—to win it? Who would hire a campaign adviser who spent time crafting a strategy to lose? From the point of view of a campaign strategist, it is not just a waste of time to think like an academic but it could also harm the campaign in concrete and practical ways. Hence, "end of story"—better not even to utter the words "sometimes it is better to lose."

Even from the perspective of political scientists and other scholars of American politics who like to utter words and entertain hypotheses, one can make a case for the face-value benefit of a focus on traditional winning. The emphasis on winning is thought to be partly responsible for the relatively moderate and stable nature of American liberal democracy. As James Ceaser has shown, the American party system was invented in the nineteenth century to make achieving office, especially presidential office, its defining goal.[14] The Founders had feared political parties because they could destabilize politics by facilitating and fueling factions devoted to alternative regimes, or to competing religions, or to fundamentally different ideological visions. Designed in the nineteenth century by Martin Van Buren, mass

American political parties would, for the most part, be different from previous parties and the factions so familiar to, and so despised by, leading American Founders. American parties could be designed to enhance and make effective a constitution thought to be incompatible with the old and familiar kinds of parties. Each composed of a broad and diverse set of factions, the American parties would compete for opportunities to hold office and would disperse to their many factions the benefits of holding office. So designed, in order to win, political parties would vie for the "center" of the spectrum of political views and thus, more often than not, would look similar to each other regarding their programmatic visions. According to this scholarly view, the desire and effort to win, in the traditional sense, induces a beneficial moderation in the political system.

For much of American history, this kind of moderate partisan order fairly characterized American politics.[15] Yet this so-called normal politics has also been the subject of criticism by pundits and even by some political scientists in the mid-twentieth century—referred to as a "tweedle dee, tweedle dum" party politics with not "a dime's worth of difference" between the two major parties.[16] The chief complaint was that, in their quest for the winning center, the parties so resembled each other that American voters lacked real choice and the opportunity to hold government accountable. Both parties had as their fundamental purpose the capture of office rather than the advancement of a political vision, and thus voters were left without a clear set of criteria by which to judge the performance of the elected party. According to this view, the emphasis on winning might be good for stable governance, but it is bad for democracy.[17]

Today, in our polarized and increasingly ideologically divided political world, one might yearn for a return to the pattern of the past, when parties, and the politicians who sought victory under their banner, brought consensus and moderation to politics. The point we want to stress, however, is that the modern mass two-party system was intentionally designed to make ambition for office—rather than advancement of political causes—the defining feature of American politics.[18] Thus, from the perspective of the polity (and some of its founders) as well as from the perspective of politicians and their advisers, it makes sense to claim that "it's always better to win than to lose" because winning was all about obtaining office. The sentiment is not only a practical maxim but also a designed and typically a salutary normative attribute of a political order.

Yet even in the long-dominant moderated partisan political order, American politics has been punctuated by moments of significant change fueled by articulated, significant differences between the major political parties. These junctures and moments of political change, including the three at the center of our analysis, show why the political operative was wrong, or at least shortsighted. It is not *always* better to win an election. If one's primary political purpose is not simply to win but to do so in order to advance an alternative vision to the status quo—to fashion a political movement, to change the constitutional order, or to defend the status quo against change—then winning is preferable to losing only if it actually advances one's primary goals. Might it not be the case that, in some circumstances, losing advances one's goals more effectively than winning the particular contest at hand? And winning in the conventional sense might mean defeat? Our answer to these questions is yes.

From a counterfactual perspective, we mean to show with our cases how it could be that winning outright in these moments of study might have meant losing in the long run. Consider the cases of Andrew Johnson and Barry Goldwater, for example. As vice president to Abraham Lincoln, Johnson succeeded to the presidency after Lincoln's assassination, and he served for just one term before being essentially chased out of office by Radical Republicans in Congress. Despite a successful career in the Senate, staunch conservative Republican Barry Goldwater suffered a disastrous loss to Lyndon Johnson in the presidential contest of 1964 and cost his party seats in Congress as well. These losses were not unforeseen. Both men knew what they were up against and were convinced that if they had adopted strategies more likely to achieve office they might have won election or reelection, or at least fared better than they did—the traditional definition of success. But they would have set their movements back, undermined the ideas that animated those movements, and thereby lost what was most important to them. Thus, if we are convincing in our argument that losing can sometimes be winning over the longer term, it also follows that political victory can sometimes mean losing over the longer term.

A superb example of this—and of the utility of rethinking success and failure—is a fine study of Brazilian presidential politics by our colleague Wendy Hunter. In her recent book, *The Transformation of the Workers' Party in Brazil, 1989–2009*, Hunter shows how a party of the left, the *Partido dos Trabalhadores* (PT), a perpetual loser in Brazilian presidential politics, was able to win and elevate its leader, Luiz Inácio Lula da Silva ("Lula") to the presidency.[19] The Workers' Party was a small and radical organization when it was founded. Its ideological commitments were firm and consistent, but they also prevented electoral success. Lula had run and lost in 1989, 1994, and 1998 before finally winning in 2002. Hunter's explanation for the eventual success is that Lula so moderated the party's positions that they became indistinguishable from centrist positions or in some instances conservative policies. Lula figured out how to forge a winning coalition by changing the political program of his party. Hunter also offers a nice account of the disaffection of the PT's core members and supporters as the basic commitments were abandoned.

There is no doubt that Lula won election, reelection in 2006, and election for his former chief of staff as his successor in 2011. If winning and holding office is the mark of success, then Hunter offers a story of a remarkable political strategy. But from the perspective of the core members and constituency of the Workers' Party, the price of that victory was the destruction of the heart and soul of the party. Can it really be said that the Workers' Party was successful if it had to adopt the policies it opposed to win office? Did it really win in the long run? Was the party that "won" still genuinely the Workers' Party?

Another example, this time drawn from the United States, is the preemptive president in Stephen Skowronek's schema of the presidency in political time.[20] In Skowronek's well-known typology, a president's behavior and success is shaped by where he falls in the cycle of partisan political regimes. While some, like Franklin D. Roosevelt, "reconstruct" American politics anew from the ashes of a previous partisan regime, most presidents (affiliated with the regime) either maintain and extend the dominant regime, or (if opposed to the regime) they try to disrupt it but fail because of the strength of the regime. These last are what Skowronek labels "preemptive presidencies," and Eisenhower, during the New Deal regime, and Clinton, during the Reagan regime, are prime examples. Both won electorally and were even reelected. Yet they did so by embracing many of the principles of the opposition party's dominant regime. Thus, Eisenhower was dismissed by conservatives opposed to the New Deal as nothing more than a "New Deal lite" president. And Clinton was decried by those on the left for selling out traditional Democratic ideas in favor of more centrist economic positions and policies. While both presidents secured victories for their parties when the political winds were unfavorable, each did so at the cost of what the party stood for in the eyes of many of its supporters. As with Lula and the Workers' Party, these examples force us to ask: Are those sorts of victories truly success stories?[21]

Thus, our inquiry into the three episodes of loss in constitutional moments has forced us to revisit common understandings of what it means to win or lose a political contest. Sometimes the visionary, programmatic, and policy objectives of a candidate and party are better served by losing a contest, if necessary, to substantively prevail in the long run. Similarly, sometimes winning a contest can be a hollow victory if it requires abandoning the political objectives around which the party is organized and sustained. Winning can be losing and, as we show in our cases, losing can be winning in the long run. There are undoubtedly many other interesting cases in American politics when this is true.

One problem with using common terms such as "winning" and "losing" that we mean to revise and complicate is that it is stylistically difficult to remind readers of these complications at every invocation. As a shorthand, we will sometimes refer to losing in the short term and winning in the long run, or vice versa. However, to argue that an actor who lost decisively in an initial electoral or legislative contest prevails in the long run need not mean that the long-run influence was decisive in all respects or that it was seamlessly successful. Similarly, an actor who wins decisively initially but is hampered in advancing his policy vision need not be losing in the long run in all respects. For these reasons, some readers of our interpretation of the Founding, Reconstruction, and the New Deal may be tempted to conclude that no one wins and no one loses because of these complications. Yet it is precisely the complications that we mean to highlight and foreground. Each antagonist in these regime-shaping contests wins in some respects and loses in others, and wins at some moments and loses at others. Mapping that complex story is a fundamental challenge for the study of American political development as well as an opportunity to rethink the vocabulary of winning, losing, success, and failure.

AGENCY

Another reason our cases are interesting is that they show how the long-term success of political loss can be more than an ironic fact. The mechanisms of loss may be a form of agency. The way political actors choose to act in the course of their initial loss can facilitate the transformation of that loss into success in the long term. We initially developed this insight in response to an invitation to a conference at Yale, organized by Stephen Skowronek, on the notion of agency in American politics.[22] Skowronek believed that decades of work in American political development had resulted in a collective overemphasis on the role of "structure" in American politics. He urged that it was time to revisit and reinvigorate the companion and competing notion of political agency. The chapter on Andrew Johnson in this book began as a response to Skowronek's invitation to think about the relationship between agency and structure.

On first consideration, we had thought to argue that Johnson was simply more successful in the long run than generally recognized. But as we deepened our research, we quickly realized that more could, and should, be said about how Johnson actually conducted himself during his presidency and how his actions reverberated in subsequent politics. We came to see that how he chose to act could account for both his initial political defeat and the subsequent influence and power of his political project. In this sense, we realized that Johnson offered a nice case of losing as a form of agency. As we explain in chapter 3, Johnson's behavior while in office is often dismissed as ill-advised, wrongheaded, incompetent, and foolish. This makes every bit of sense if his goal was simply his own political survival. It also makes sense from a normative standpoint that takes seriously the liberal constitutional commitment to equality. But from the vantage of someone who strove to prosecute a political and policy agenda under the most adverse of circumstances, when outright success was clearly impossible, his behaviors look far more rational—aimed at constructing a foundation, rhetorical and otherwise, for the fight to continue, and succeed, down the proverbial road. In our chapter, we show how Johnson developed and acted upon a truly original conception of leadership. Instead of a politics of compromise and bargaining in the conventional senses, he developed a strategy of obstruction, preemption, and ideological revision that provided a foundation for restoration, rather than reconstruction, of the southern political establishment. The choices he made, and the agency that he exercised in doing so, ensured his immediate political defeat yet also enabled the long-term and lasting success of his vision.

The mechanisms of loss were very different for the Anti-Federalists and somewhat different for Barry Goldwater, but in both cases the way loss was conducted facilitated the eventual long-term influence and success of the defeated political projects. In the 1964 campaign, Goldwater was surrounded by political advisers for whom winning the presidential election was the primary goal and the most significant marker of success. They urged the senator to moderate his views and to revise his public persona in ways that would attract more votes. Goldwater adamantly resisted all of these efforts and instead adopted strategies and language suited to organize, inspire, and expand a conservative movement. The same language, positions, campaign decisions, and personal style that facilitated the promotion of his conservative vision undermined his chances in the general election for president of the United States. Lyndon Baines Johnson, while always the clear favorite in the aftermath of Kennedy's assassination, won by such a large margin that some of his supporters initially thought he had irrevocably set back the conservative movement as well. But recent scholarship on the rise of conservatism has provided considerable support for our argument that it is the way Goldwater lost that made possible Ronald Reagan's later ascendance. In chapter 4, we show that the manner in which Goldwater conducted his presidential campaign fortified the conservative movement for future success, persuaded other Republican leaders to jettison moderation, and primed a national audience to eventually reject many attributes of New Deal liberalism. We call Goldwater's agency an example of the politics of integrity, and it enabled eventual repudiation of the New Deal regime along with conservative success.

Perhaps the most interesting case of agency is that of the Anti-Federalists. In an attempt to defeat ratification of the Constitution, the Anti-Federalists articulated the Federalist case for the political trajectory of the proposed new constitution more clearly and more frankly than did the Federalists. They showed the proposal to be what it was: a radical departure from the status quo. In order to blunt this attack, the Federalists initially denied the radical nature of the proposal, and they crafted a rhetoric designed to assuage fears and to appeal to voters with Anti-Federal sentiments. After downplaying the novelty of the Constitution's proposed governing arrangements, Federalists subsequently shifted to a promotion of the plan that conceded in a sophisticated manner the Anti-Federalist's critical description. The Constitution was adopted in what can only be described as a monumental win for the Federalists and a huge loss for their opponents. However, as the new regime was established, Anti-Federalists and the heirs to their political persuasion effectively used the early defensive rhetoric of *The Federalist* to reinterpret and subvert the Federalist political project. We call this form of agency the politics of appropriation. In this case, the initial actions of the losers forced the "winners" to adopt strategies to win votes that then provided the very resources needed to subvert the "winning" political project. Put differently, Anti-Federalists' efforts to defeat ratification unintentionally provoked a Federalist rhetorical response that they and their heirs then, intentionally, appropriated in order to recover—and succeed with—their early aims. This process was so thorough and yet so subtle that most people today fail to recognize that what they think are Federalist ideas actually manifest the Anti-Federal project to subvert the Constitution by reintroducing into it the animating concepts of the Articles of Confederation. Thus, many who believe that they are celebrating the Constitution with unreflective paeans to limited government are fortifying the sentiment of the Constitution's original enemies. This is a truly complex yet fascinating case of political agency on the part of Anti-Federalists and their heirs in the early republic.

In each of these cases, the actors who interest us chose to engage in political acts and used rhetoric that led to their defeat, yet these very actions and rhetoric also facilitated the eventual success of their programs. Despite these similarities, the first case of the Anti-Federalists is different from the other two. The battle was over a constitution that, once ratified, set the parameters within which the subsequent two contests in our study were undertaken. Critically, the eventual success of the Anti-Federalists included providing rhetorical resources for our subsequent losers, Johnson and Goldwater, and others to use in their efforts to achieve their agendas. Thus, by developing and ensuring the incorporation of key constitutional rhetoric (at odds with the Federalists' constitutional intentions, as we show in chapter 2), Anti-Federalists helped to enable and fortify Johnson and Goldwater in their efforts, giving both men reason to believe in the legitimacy of their causes and assistance in their efforts to persuade others. In this way, the constitutional rhetoric of the Anti-Federalists both became a resource for and was repurposed by Johnson, and this then again by Goldwater. Recognizing the rhetorical lineage and the strategic redeployments is crucial to understanding the sustenance of the illiberal tradition and the agency of the political leaders who contributed to it.

Some might reasonably wonder whether one can be sure that the Anti-Federalists, Johnson, and Goldwater caused the subsequent influence of their policies. It can, of course, be argued that policies like those that these leaders preferred later prevailed for reasons having nothing to do with them, that these sorts of outcomes would have developed for reasons other than the actions of the leaders themselves. It is impossible to know whether the actions of these leaders were *necessary* conditions for the later emergence of policies that resembled their visions. But one can never prove that any leader was necessary for the articulation and success of policies that he or she advanced. This challenge is an inevitable feature of the "great man" claims about history more generally, but rarely are the more conventionally celebrated leaders disregarded because of it. No one questions, for example, whether Franklin D. Roosevelt influenced the success of the New Deal order, even while most acknowledge the influence of other factors. Our aim here is simply to show that—as is often plausibly argued for the Federalists, Abraham Lincoln, and FDR—the Anti-Federalists, Johnson, and Goldwater may also have influenced the subsequent success of the ideas they promoted.

Reconstitution

In each of the three chapters that follow this one we reveal a process of reversal, and we show the agency involved in the transformation of loss into success. For us, the variety of actors, conditions, strategies, and, indeed, successes that our depiction yields is fascinating in its own right. In the richness of their variety, these cases suggest a complex relationship between loss and success, and each requires us to expand, in slightly different ways, our definition of what it means to lose and to succeed. We develop these themes in chapter 5.

Our concluding chapter is also devoted to discussion of a larger, macrohistorical dynamic that we believe our cases, taken together, illuminate, and that is the animating purpose of our study. In this discussion, we connect arguments about change with disputes about the character of the American regime. Earlier, we briefly described the view of scholars who see American history as a series of disruptive changes followed by periods of normalcy. The weight and significance of these "constitutional moments" is such that those who write about them almost always depict America as a country of successive regimes. We show how, on the one hand, major partisan disruptions have not been equivalent to true regime change, yet on the other hand, more disruption has been induced by political contestation than scholars of American political development have acknowledged.

By nuancing the story of progressive regime changes, our account also forces a revision of the depiction of American politics as "exceptional," distinguishable from other modern, industrial democracies for its basis in a set of liberal ideas, its creed. In that picture of overall liberal continuity, political conflict stems from periodic distances between the practices on the ground and the ideals of the creed. Others have suggested that we actually resemble those other modern democracies, because the creed has simply camouflaged the extent to which we do have traditional conflicts between those who are included and those who are excluded, or between the haves and have-nots. Our account shows how adherence to the creed has been advanced while an alternative tradition of ascriptive hierarchy has simultaneously been sustained, and how, by thinking in conventional terms about winning and losing, observers have missed the historical braiding of these two traditions that has helped to nourish hierarchies.

In the last chapter, we discuss the best versions of these dominant synoptic pictures of change and continuity. The pictures are not wrong. There is some truth to both of these images. But they are also misleading. We then supplement sophisticated renditions of the two main synoptic perspectives with our own account of the complex dynamic revealed by the legacy of loss in American politics. Our own picture will be clearer once the reader has the details of our cases in mind. However, we can say here that against the continuity of a conscious creed, we locate continuity in an unrecognized political logic of the Constitution. This often unnoticed political logic, which we describe in chapter 2, is the foundational layer of American political development. In chapters 3 and 4, we redescribe the well-known liberal and conservative traditions as a complex inheritance from the original founding debate over the *merits* of that political logic. Our findings in chapters 2, 3, and 4, sometimes surprising and counterintuitive, inform our discussion in chapter 5 where we return to an explicit reflection on the major synoptic perspectives on American politics. In contrast to a symmetrical dialogue between well-defined liberal and antiliberal traditions, we see less coherent traditions with dominant and subsidiary strands. The liberal tradition sometimes generates illiberal practices, while the antiliberal tradition sometimes features liberal or, better said, constitutional, elements. In chapter 5, we relabel these liberal and ascriptive traditions as constitutional and anticonstitutional. Because the constitutional and anticonstitutional normative traditions borrow from each other, our metaphor for their place in American political development is a four-strand braid. Though mixing metaphors, we find it helpful to depict this braid as layered over the unnoticed but enduring political logic of the constitutional order.

Founding
The Anti-Federal Appropriation

Lamenting the 2012 Supreme Court ruling that upheld the mandate for individuals to purchase health insurance in the Patient Protection and Affordable Care Act (otherwise known as "Obamacare"), Peggy Noonan built her *Wall Street Journal* column around this key quotation from the dissenting opinion of Justices Scalia, Kennedy, Thomas, and Alito: "If Congress can reach out and command even those furthest removed from an interstate market to participate in the market, then the Commerce Clause becomes a font of unlimited power or, in Hamilton's words, 'the hideous monster whose devouring jaws . . . spare neither sex nor age, nor high nor low, nor sacred nor profane.'"[1] These words from *Federalist* No. 33 capture well the dissenting justices' understanding of the unconstitutionality of the individual mandate. Moreover, because Chief Justice John Roberts in his majority opinion agreed with the dissenters that the Commerce Clause did not authorize the individual mandate (finding authority for it in the taxing power instead), this "dissenting view" is actually part of the winning coalition that established what is now the new Supreme Court doctrine regarding the meaning of the Commerce Clause.[2]

The quotation marks a dramatic change in the post–New Deal political order signaling a new legal skepticism about the reach of national power to regulate commerce. The justices and the journalist do not seem to realize, however, that Hamilton did not agree with the words that they quote so approvingly. Hamilton is clear that those sentiments are not his own. Rather, they were the "exaggerated colors of misrepresentation" advanced by "virulent" and "petulant" Anti-Federalists. Hamilton actually devotes *Federalist* No. 33 to showing why they were wrong.[3]

Moreover, Hamilton was not discussing the Commerce Clause but rather was describing the Anti-Federalist reaction to the Necessary and Proper Clause and the Supremacy Clause and their implications for the national government's power to tax. As noted, John Roberts upheld the individual mandate with a broad reading of the power to tax. The Anti-Federalists may have shared the dissenting justices' political sensibility about the evils of "big government," but both the Anti-Federalists and the Federalists agreed with Justice Roberts's understanding of the meaning of the Constitution's taxing power.

The misquotation of *The Federalist* in one of the most important Supreme Court cases of our time is stunning. It deserves derision with words as colorful as those that Justice Scalia wielded so inaccurately. It is a form of intellectual and constitutional fraud. But it is much more. It is a revealing example of how the Anti-Federalist movement transformed its profound defeat in the battle over ratification of the Constitution into a viable and legitimate strand of constitutional interpretation that has been sustained across the major turning points of American political life. So memorable is the loss and so thorough was the transformation that Anti-Federalist authorship of a dominant interpretation of the Constitution is typically miscredited, as it was in this instance, to the Federalists. This recent court case illustrates our argument that the legitimation of Anti-Federalist thinking in American political life was accomplished through the appropriation, by Anti-Federalists and their heirs, of rhetoric used in *The Federalist* during ratification to mute the original Anti-Federalist critique of the proposed constitution. This complex process of rhetorical appropriation has fundamentally shaped American political development, yet it is largely unrecognized and, as a result, the true aims of the most articulate and influential founding proposers of the Constitution are regularly miscast. In utterances and writings, justices like Clarence Thomas and Antonin Scalia, and many conservatives before them, claim—and no doubt believe—that they are restoring the Constitution to its original Federalist roots. They seem not to realize that they are allies of the social movement that was opposed to the Constitution of the United States. What precisely is the source of this extraordinary misunderstanding? What have been its consequences for American political development? What are the legacies of the first major loss in American political history?

In the sections that follow we first develop our general claim that the very mechanisms used by the Anti-Federalists in their failed effort to defeat the Constitution made possible their subsequent significant success in informing constitutional interpretation. We describe a three-step process of rhetorical articulation. First, during the battle over constitutional ratification, Anti-Federalists levied charges against the proposed Constitution. Second, as a politically prudent response given the gravity of the charges and the unfavorable political context, the Federalists deployed rhetoric that downplayed their ambitions before shifting to a subtle defense of those very same ambitions. Third, and finally, after the Federalists' ratification victory, Anti-Federalists and their heirs in the new constitutional regime strategically appropriated the initial, mollifying rhetoric of the Federalists to make a persuasive argument for a particular interpretation of the Constitution, gaining authority and influence through attribution of this view to the Federalists.

We then illustrate and elaborate this argument with examples of two major areas of contention during ratification debates. In the debates over federalism and the separation of powers, Anti-Federalists uncovered the logic of the proposed Constitution and attacked its implications as radical and dangerous departures from existing political practices. The Federalist strategy was first to reassure a skeptical citizenry by minimizing the departure that the proposed Constitution represented and then, in subsequent iterations of their argument, to defend the benefits of the Constitution in ways that reveal the true extent of the changes that they were, in fact, proposing. The overstatement in the initial Federalist iteration, that the features of the proposed regime were similar to current practices, was certainly useful—and probably necessary—to secure ratification by an anxious, postrevolutionary population. Yet that language provided the authoritative foundation upon which Anti-Federalists and their political heirs successfully reinterpreted the Constitution after ratification. Modern proponents of national government strength or robust executive power occasionally reference *The Federalist*'s later, stronger case for the administrative state. But more often, the iterations of *The Federalist*'s argument are missed and forgotten and the later, stronger case is rebutted with invocations of the earlier mollifying rhetoric.

The successful resurrection of the initially defeated Anti-Federalist ideas was made possible through a rhetorical appropriation of the Federalist defense of the Constitution. The Anti-Federalists may not have initially intended this because they planned to defeat ratification. Yet, subsequent to the initial ratification campaign, the Anti-Federalists and their political heirs certainly acted purposefully and strategically when deploying the Federalists' own rhetoric against the constitutional project. They sought to reclaim through interpretation what they had lost through constitutional construction and ratification. The Anti-Federal success with this act of appropriation has obscured its true origins, and their creative reinterpretation of *The Federalist*'s defense of the Constitution has been associated with an antistatist strand of political action ever since.

The very robustness of the Anti-Federalist success helped to shape the loss-to-success outcomes witnessed in our subsequent two cases by providing and legitimating the rhetorical resources that both Andrew Johnson and Barry Goldwater used in their own battles to reconstitute the American regime. Understanding this first legacy of loss is thus instrumental to understanding later legacies, and, as we argue in chapter 5, to appreciating the significance of regime antimoments in sustaining the antiliberal tradition in American politics.

The Ratification Battle—Huge Win, Huge Loss

It is hard to overstate how much was at stake in America's first national campaign, and although the story is familiar, it is helpful to review some highlights in order to appreciate the enormity of the Federalist ratification victory. Commissioned to revise the Articles of Confederation, delegates to the Philadelphia convention in 1787 abandoned their charge. By the terms of the Articles, they acted illegally. They did not propose amendments to be ratified according to the procedures of the Articles but instead proposed an entirely new regime to be authorized by new procedures that they also designed—not by the legal forms of the regime that commissioned them. Under the Articles, amendments would have required unanimous approval of all of the legislatures of the states in the union. The proposed new Constitution would not be presented to any of the state legislatures for ratification but instead to specially elected conventions in each state. Only nine of these ratifying conventions, rather than all thirteen state legislatures, would be required to establish this new regime. This proposal was audacious in many respects, not the least of which was the frank acknowledgment that a constitutional revolution was being set in motion whose fate was put in the hands of ordinary citizens and their specially elected delegates.[4]

The Philadelphia convention chose not to camouflage the significance of the change that was being proposed. The change could not be honestly captured in "amendments" to the Articles because the proposed changes went to the very heart of the old regime; they were so significant that by the terms of the old regime they would have been "unconstitutional" constitutional amendments even if approval for them in that form could have been secured.[5] The defect of the Articles was that the shared central authority lacked the power necessary to accomplish its responsibilities because it depended on the states for resources. Under the Articles, the states retained true sovereignty and the so-called central government responsible for defense and other shared concerns was answerable to each state government. The so-called constitution of the confederation was actually more like a treaty with real constitutional authority residing in each of the thirteen states. The proponents of the new Constitution argued that the central government under the Articles was not actually a government at all. They proposed to repair that defect by establishing a direct and unmediated relation between the new national authority and ordinary citizens.

Less generally appreciated is the fact that the new Constitution represented a plan for a new way of life, not just a new arrangement of power. Although during the ratification debate the Anti-Federalists never fully theorized an agrarian ideal, it was implicit in what they did argue.[6] The Constitution would replace a republican ideal of smaller, homogeneous communities in which commerce was wedded to agriculture, with a regime of continental dimension, a commercial republic in which agriculture would play a supporting role.[7] The manners, mores, habits, and culture of the regime would be fundamentally altered as a result. In other words, the Constitution proposed a revolution in the design of a whole polity—new forms of living as well as new forms of governance.[8]

This was neither an ordinary election nor an ordinary political campaign. Proponents of such massive change required many crucial smaller victories. As mentioned above, they needed to change the agenda of the drafting convention and the procedures that governed their own work. They needed to persuade the state legislatures to set up the special ratifying conventions that supplanted the legislatures' own authority.[9] They needed to succeed in at least nine of thirteen separate campaigns, a process of "labyrinthine complexity. . . . Each state made its own rules about the number, apportionment, and manner of choosing delegates, the result being that the approximately 1,750 men who sat in the several conventions were selected in hundreds of largely uncoordinated elections, mainly by town meetings in New England and by countywide polls elsewhere. Moreover, the process unfolded over a period of almost three years."[10]

During the ratification debate, the proponents and opponents of ratification resembled social movements or coalitions of interests rather than organized political parties. The coalition that emerged to write and organize in opposition to the Constitution was large and diverse. At its core were delegates who preferred the old regime, perhaps modified, to a new one. They were joined by some who were open to a new regime but not the one proposed, and by others who liked the one proposed but had deep misgivings about some aspect of it. The opponents included men who had walked out of the drafting convention and who were prepared to cast doubt on its legitimacy given the abandonment of existing political and legal procedures. While they were a diverse group of individuals with differences in ideas and strategies, they *became* united, as Anti-Federalists, in their opposition to the ratification of the Constitution just as a very diverse group of Federalists *became* united on behalf of ratification.[11]

Among the coalition of opponents were delegates who were open to approval of the new Constitution contingent on the adoption of amendments. Proponents of the Constitution, however, needed to defeat any and all amendments—those that might subvert the Constitution's fundamental principles as well as those that were ancillary and more benign—because in a process as complicated as that being undertaken, "contingent" approval would, as a practical matter, mean defeat of the Constitution. No matter how you slice it, the hurdles to creating and ratifying the Constitution were immense.

Yet, the Federalists won the ratification fight, and the Anti-Federalists lost. The Constitution was ratified by the necessary nine states fairly quickly between December 1787 and June 1788. There followed a very close battle in the large state of Virginia, where James Madison narrowly secured ratification (89 to 79) by convincing enough delegates that the new union advanced the sectional interests of the South. The vote in New York was even closer (30 to 27), but passage in this state made it the eleventh one to ratify. After the First Congress under the new Constitution passed the Bill of Rights, North Carolina, where ratification had been rejected initially, called a second convention and joined the union. Recalcitrant Rhode Island, the original and most tenacious holdout, finally allowed a convention to be called in May 1790 where ratification was secured by the slim margin of 34 to 32. The Federalist victory was thus, eventually, complete with all thirteen states ratifying the Constitution.[12]

It is conventional scholarly wisdom that while the Federalists won the battle for the Constitution, the Anti-Federalists were victorious in securing the Bill of Rights. Given that most Americans' understanding of the Constitution today is limited to portions of the Bill of Rights, it might be argued that here is very good evidence that the Anti-Federalists indeed were the bigger victors in the long run. While there is some truth to this observation (and we return to this point in the concluding chapter), we note here that when the Bill of Rights was crafted and adopted in the First Congress of the United States, it was a major victory for the Federalists and yet another loss for the Anti-Federalists. During the Massachusetts ratifying convention, Anti-Federalists were mollified by John Hancock's proposal to recommend amending the Constitution in the First Congress to include the Bill of Rights. This was a breakthrough for the Federalist effort because it meant that ratification in Massachusetts was not made contingent on this "recommendation," which had been the strategy of the opponents of ratification. While ratification *contingent* on amendments would have opened up a Pandora's box and meant near certain defeat of the proposed Constitution, *recommended* amendments advanced the Federalist cause. The Massachusetts compromise paved the way for ratification in subsequent states.

The First Congress of the United States was composed of a very large majority of Federalists in both the House and the

Senate. James Madison urged the Congress to make good on the promise to Massachusetts and other states to add a bill of rights even though there was other important business to settle in establishing a new government and there were few supporters of amendment among his colleagues. Madison pressed forward because he feared that to renege on that ratification commitment would open the door for harmful amendments when the political tide turned and former opponents to ratification controlled the legislature or, even worse, when sentiment crystallized in favor of a second constitutional convention. He realized that the main objective of the Anti-Federalists was not to secure the sorts of individual rights now contained in the Bill of Rights but rather to advance structural amendments to change the most fundamental features of the Constitution and thereby restore power to the states.[13] To thwart this possibility, Madison and his Federalist colleagues adopted a bill of rights that contained amendments that were different from those the Anti-Federalists preferred. As Herbert J. Storing argued, "Madison's insistent sponsorship of amendments has to be seen as the final step in the strikingly successful Federalist strategy to secure an effective national government."[14]

The ratification of the Constitution was a stunning Federalist political victory both in the extent of the political transformation that it set in motion and in the extraordinary number of obstacles that it needed to overcome along the way. And it was a thoroughgoing loss for those who wished to preserve the previous regime or who were, at least, opposed to the Federalist plan. What accounts for this victory and this loss? We don't presume to canvass the myriad factors that contributed to these results. This is ground well-trod by historians and there is much excellent scholarship on this topic; we encourage interested readers to begin with Pauline Maier's superb book, which covers much of this territory.[15] She points out, for example, that the Federalists owned most of the newspapers, controlled the circulation of much of the debate, and indeed suppressed many dissenting publications. They were the agenda setters and had the advantage of defending a positive vision, a proposal, whereas the opponents of the Constitution were required to present their vision negatively, through the rejection of the proposal. More important, the reasons for Federalist victory vary from state to state because the politics specific to each state campaign were distinctive. With the recent publication of the *Documentary History of the Ratification Campaign*, scholars are only now beginning to map the complex political story that unfolded state by state.[16]

We wish to highlight and analyze one crucial factor that transcended the specifics of each state: Federalist rhetoric and manner of argumentation. Over the course of the entire campaign, the Federalists developed an ability to allay the fears of ordinary citizens that change would be too much to bear. They overcame the natural and normal conservative responses of a citizenry faced with a new and unfamiliar proposal in a time fraught with uncertainty. One can see this assuaging strategy in the most basic framing of the debate—the naming of the two partisan positions. Up until this point, we have referred to the Anti-Federalists as "opponents of ratification" because they did not choose that name for themselves. The Federalists chose their own name as well as the label of their opponents. Unlike the Philadelphia convention, which in its formal proposal was clear and frank in presenting the new Constitution as a fundamental change from the past, the Federalist campaign for ratification was more deliberate and circumspect in making the case for the nationalizing trajectory of the new Constitution. It attempted to win support by initially interpreting the Constitution as an improvement of the familiar rather than as the inauguration of something unprecedented and new. Over time, Federalists embraced and defended the newness of their project, but initially they prepared the ground for change by arguing that the proposal was merely an improvement of known political institutions and practices. Their sober caution was a response to Anti-Federalist rhetoric that stressed the Constitution as a radical (and in their view a dangerous) departure from time-tested political practices.

Thus, the Federalists began their campaign by claiming for

their own name the constitutive principle of the opposition. Before the attacks on the Constitution as a project of national consolidation could be articulated, the proponents of the new regime named themselves Federalists. The more accurate labeling of the partisans in the ratification debate would have been "nationalists" for the proponents of the new Constitution and "federalists" for the opponents, those generally dedicated to preserving greater state power in a federal system.[17] Yet the Federalists made sure that this was not to be, successfully claiming for themselves the federalist label while casting their opponents as "anti-federalists." So successful was this taking of nomenclature that the meaning of the appropriated word was altered. Today, we think of the national government as the "federal" government. The Federalists succeeded in stealing the proper name of their opponents and at the same time burdened them with a label that cast them negatively, indeed as naysayers of their own fundamental identity.

The rhetoric of naming or of labels also illustrates our central thesis—Federalist rhetorical choices that facilitated their stunning victory (or contributed to Anti-Federalist defeat) at the same time provided resources for the political heirs of the Anti-Federalist movement to modify, if not subvert, the American constitutional order secured by Federalists. Naming themselves "federalists" to advance a nationalist constitutional project provided a potent resource for subsequent partisans who opposed the development of the administrative state and other exercises of national power. The heirs to the Anti-Federalists could claim that the Constitution had departed from the intentions of its victorious founders by holding them to their word that they were "federalists," not nationalists, and that the regime was at core federal, not national.[18]

David J. Siemers and Jack Rakove have noticed that *The Federalist* gained authoritative status due to the irony that under the new Constitution, the former Anti-Federalists "were able to use Publius as an ally in the fight against those who would extend federal authority."[19] Siemers persuasively shows how the Anti-

Federalists played a crucial role in the legitimation of the Federalist constitution by lending their support to it immediately upon ratification. In other words, by this logic and to rephrase Jefferson's famous declaration, everyone was a federalist now. In this chapter, we develop the other side of that coin. The Anti-Federalists did not decide to support the Constitution after ratification because they wanted to legitimize the Federalist project (even if their initial actions had that effect). Rather, after ratification, the Anti-Federalists adopted a new strategy to accomplish their old purposes, and they bequeathed this strategy to their political heirs. Most thoughtful Anti-Federalists had agreed the Articles of Confederation needed to be repaired, that they faced a crisis of governance. They opposed the Constitution in favor of a return to the original plan to amend and improve the Articles. In the post-ratification political world, the Anti-Federalist strategy became one of appropriating language in *The Federalist* in order to reinterpret the Constitution so that it worked differently from the way originally planned. They sought to recover the spirit of the Articles in a reinterpreted Constitution. They began a tradition of constitutional interpretation at odds with the animating political logic of the Constitution—a logic they had previously described so well as one that would bring forth a national regime and a new polity. We mean to show how the Anti-Federalist critique of the proposed Constitution compelled a response from *The Federalist*, prompting a rhetorical structure that ultimately was used to legitimate this Anti-Federal political persuasion, facilitating an opposing political and interpretative tradition layered over the constitutive logic of the Constitution. With *The Federalist* as their authority, Anti-Federalists and their political heirs could legitimately pursue a vision of the American order that competed with, and sometimes subverted, the political logic of the Constitution.

These two conflicting aspects of American political development took root in the founding era and have persisted throughout American history. The very same strategic decisions that facilitated the massive victory of the Federalists in the face of strong Anti-Federalist critique and an uncertain political climate then enabled an opposing Anti-Federal tradition more vibrant and more problematic for the regime than most scholars have noticed. In other words, it was the politically expedient early rhetoric of *The Federalist* that helped turn the biggest losers in American politics, the Anti-Federalists, into winners over the long run.

Federalists and Anti-Federalists

One good result of the recent resurgence of scholarship on the American founding period is that it has brought attention to the outpouring of political writing that shaped the ratification struggle. The most influential political actors and political writings in the midst of the battle were not the texts that have achieved iconic status in American history. *The Federalist*, for example, was not widely read outside of New York. Some of the finest Anti-Federalist writing, such as "Brutus," had limited influence upon publication. Nevertheless, it is appropriate, indeed essential, to focus on these texts if the long-term success of the Anti-Federal movement is to be understood. Some political texts achieve "iconic status" not because they express typical or common sentiments of the time in which they were written but because they display acute understanding of the issues at work. As Herbert Storing has written, they reveal not so much what was "common" as what was "fundamental."[20] To say that writers of such texts are smarter than the typical pamphleteer is to suggest that they see "farther or better," and that they can "explain more." They can explain how the Constitution will actually work, in practice and over time. They can explain how the Constitution will transform a political world, what the broad trajectory of political development will be. They paint a very plausible picture of the political future. These are not the ways ordinary citizens think and talk in the midst of political controversy. Consequently, these farseeing writings sometimes had little direct influence on the politics of their time, but they did have enormous influence on politics in the future—an influence signaled and facilitated by their "iconic status." Thus, *The Federalist* and major Anti-Federal writings such as essays by "Brutus" and "The Federal Farmer" are routinely cited in searches for the Constitution's "original meaning" regardless of whether many citizens in the founding era understood or agreed with the views they express.[21] Our method of analysis in this chapter follows Storing in relying on these "iconic" texts as an indication of the animating concerns of the Federalists and Anti-Federalists, even while we acknowledge the diversity of arguments and fears expressed, especially among the Anti-Federalists. For the purpose of political analysis, we proceed differently from many historians of the period for whom the task is to render a complete account of the founding era. While we profit greatly from their accounts, our task is distinct, a form of political interpretation similar to Storing's. To understand the meaning and consequences of founding decisions and to unpack the source and character of contending traditions in American political thought, it is more fruitful for us to focus on the atypical, iconic texts that became powerful resources for subsequent regime-shaping contests than to map the common or typical sentiments of the entire mass of Federalist and Anti-Federal writings.[22]

The Federalist and leading Anti-Federalists shared a view of constitutional interpretation that is strikingly different from conventional approaches today, including the views of those who invoke them. Conservatives in contemporary America tether constitutional meaning to specific clauses, to the meaning of the text as deduced from eighteenth-century usages and practices, and to the so-called intentions of the framers—that is, the framers (and/or the ratifiers) or the eighteenth-century people's preferences or expectations regarding the meaning of vague concepts in the document. Liberals often share these interpretative practices even when they seem to depart from them with claims that a "living Constitution" needs to be updated to contend with new and unanticipated modern circumstances. Liberals, nonetheless, pay homage to the conservative view that the original Constitution's meaning is tethered to the extant understandings and practices of the eighteenth century. The Constitution needs to be updated, in the liberal reading, because it was made for a polity that no longer exists.

Thoughtful Federalists and Anti-Federalists had a very different view of the nature of the Constitution and of the proper way to understand its meaning. For them, the document was not simply a political settlement of their own disputes regarding the shape of their government. It was also, and more importantly, an architectural plan for the building of a whole polity—government, society, culture, and even the characters of the individuals who would be its citizens. They thought of the Constitution as a plan for the future, not just a settlement for their own time. At their best, thoughtful partisans on both sides of the debate shared an approach to understanding the Constitution. One could call that approach a constitutional frame of mind or a constitutional way of thinking. Thinking constitutionally meant (1) identifying which decisions embedded in the Constitution were core and which were peripheral or ancillary; (2) elucidating the philosophic or normative presuppositions behind the core commitments; and (3) detailing the institutional, policy, and cultural implications of the core commitments. For our purposes, the identified core decisions and commitments and their political implications are the aspects of constitutional thinking most relevant to the shape of American political development.

A close look at the major aspects of the new Constitution (federalism—the relation of the states and national government; the scope of national power; the extent of executive power; the role of the judiciary; the projected shape of the economy and political culture) shows that the Anti-Federalists often described a Federalist future more vividly than did the Federalists. Anti-Federalists objected to the Constitution because they could envision the kind of polity that it would incubate and bring into being over time. As Storing has written about the Anti-Federalists,

"They did not fail to see the opportunity for American nation-hood that the Federalists seized so gloriously, but they could not join in grasping it."[23]

Anti-Federalists highlighted and worried about the implications of fundamentally new political commitments: for example, the commitment to a very big regime—a polity of continental scope; the commitment to substantial power at the national level with coercive power over individuals; the privileging of commerce in an economy of enormous geographical and demographic scope rather than multiple nodes of agriculturally based economies of modest size; and the abandoned commitment to civic education in populations of modest size and relative homogeneity. The Anti-Federalists understood that the specific provisions supportive of states in the new Constitution (equal representation in the Senate, for example) would be overwhelmed by the self-perpetuating workings of a large national regime fueled by the core commitments. Over time, they feared, the regime would become one "consolidated" national regime. And because there was no precedent for a successful democracy that massive in human history, the Anti-Federalists worried that individual rights would be insecure and indeed threatened altogether by the likelihood of governmental tyranny.[24]

The idea that the Constitution would lead to a bad form of politics was vigorously disputed by *The Federalist*. But it is vital that we separate this well-known and often studied normative dispute—whether the plausible future polity was good or bad—from the first question of what the Constitution meant, what its words implied, what its structure portended in broad nonnormative, empirical terms. On this question of *political and constitutional logic*, there was broad agreement between *The Federalist* and Anti-Federalists. Both sides understood that adoption of the Constitution meant the nationalization of American politics, "big government," a powerful presidency, and a judiciary at the national level with wide interpretative license, for example. Anti-Federalists warned of the dangers of centralized power, of a standing army, of the nationalization of policy, and of an administrative state—in short, they warned against adopting the Constitution. Federalists defended the benefits of these very same features. Both sides, therefore, agreed on what the fundamental features of the regime would be. They disagreed over its merits, not over its logic.

How then did the political heirs of the Anti-Federalists succeed in convincing many Americans, including many scholars, politicians, and Supreme Court justices as well as ordinary citizens, that "big government," the nationalization of policy, and other features of modern governance in America are *departures* from the Constitution since the Anti-Federalists so acutely and accurately described this very Constitution? They were able to do so because the Anti-Federalists had induced Federalists to defend the Constitution in ways that muted its logic. To be clear, Anti-Federalists do not launch their critique with an "end game" of winning by first losing. They intended to defeat ratification outright. Yet when they failed, by virtue of how they were made to fail—the Federalists' use of muting rhetoric—they were able to reorganize for eventual success, and this was intentional. Early regime Anti-Federalists as well as their political heirs appropriated the defensive rhetoric of the authoritative *The Federalist* to press an antistatist interpretation of the Constitution. At odds with the Federalists' constitutional aims, this interpretation was nonetheless legitimized by reference to *The Federalist*, and because of this, a powerful rhetorical strategy was available to be wielded by later political actors, Andrew Johnson and Barry Goldwater among them, as they resisted and partially thwarted the political logic, or trajectory, of the Constitution.

FEDERALISM AND STATES' RIGHTS

The animating and persistent concern of the Anti-Federalists was that the Constitution would create a new national regime, one that consolidated power in a central government, thus making state and local governments less and less relevant over time. They understood the fundamental project of the Constitution to be a nationalizing one, and this was an abandonment of the core confederal principles of the Articles. "Federalism means that the states are primary, that they are equal, and that they possess the main weight of political power. The defense of the federal character of the American union was the most prominent article of Anti-Federalist conservative doctrine."[25] Evidence of the Federalists' nationalizing commitments that fueled the Anti-Federalist worry included the letter George Washington sent to the president of the Congress with the transmittal of the proposed Constitution, in which he explicitly referred to the object of the plan as "the consolidation of our Union."[26] The Constitution established a direct and unmediated relation between the new federal government and individual citizens, bypassing the states, and this central government was given enormous power, including the powers to tax (to provide for the common defense as well as for the general welfare), to borrow money, to regulate commerce, to promote the progress of science and the useful arts, to declare war, and to call up state militias—as well as all powers necessary and proper to execute those and other powers listed elsewhere in the Constitution. The Anti-Federalists' chief complaint was that the new Constitution had replaced a regime in which the states were sovereign entities with one in which the central authority was sovereign and the states, over time, would lose sovereignty in any meaningful sense.[27]

The Federalist first attempted to mollify Anti-Federalist fears that the new constitution was a radical departure from the status quo. Publius claimed that while it was true that "federalism," understood as state sovereignty with delegations of power from the states to a central authority for common purposes, had not worked, it was not true that "nationalism" or consolidation was replacing federalism. Instead, a new kind of federalism was being invented, in which sovereignty would be shared by dividing the spheres of responsibility between states and a central authority. The old federalism was a "federation" and the new federalism would be based on a division of powers between levels of government. According to this view, the new government was a new form of mixed regime, with state and national authority shared in complicated ways that made it impossible to describe the regime as either a states' rights or a nationalist polity.

The most elaborate description of this new mixed regime was presented by Madison in *Federalist* No. 39. There he suggested dissecting aspects of politics into five categories: (1) the relation of the government to the foundation on which it was established; (2) the sources from which ordinary powers are to be drawn; (3) the operation of ordinary powers of the central government; (4) the extent of powers of the central government, and (5) the authority for changing or amending the Constitution. With respect to the first category, Madison argued that the ratification of the Constitution in conventions in each state rather than by a majority of the people in the nation as a whole made the foundation federal, not national. Because the proposed legislature would be drawn from two sources, the House elected by "the people of America" would be national in character while the Senate would represent states equally, evidencing a federal composition. The complicated selection process for the president was described as also partaking of both national and federal features, giving it a mixed character—which would also be the summary description of the sources of all the central government's ordinary powers. Madison next described the *operation* of these powers as fully national because they reach to citizens directly. But he considered the *extent* of these powers to be "federal" because they are limited to those enumerated. Finally, Madison saw the amendment procedure as partly federal and partly national because it requires a supermajority, on the one hand, but less than unanimity of the states, on the other. The whole account in *Federalist* No. 39 is a very elaborate scheme designed to reinforce the view that the newly invented form of "federalism" combines states' rights and nationalist principles.

The Anti-Federalists were not reassured by these sorts of complicated arguments. Much like Tocqueville's critique of the Aristotelian theory of "mixed regimes," they insightfully pointed out that in politics one cannot mix or share sovereignty, because one element of the mixture always dominates.[28] In their view, the

gestures to state sovereignty in the Constitution only camouflaged the fact that the national government is the predominant
power. They focused their attention on how the provisions of
the Constitution would work in practice as well as on which of
the provisions were most important. Brutus warned, for example,
that the exercise of power inherent in the necessary and proper
clause could lead the national government to "annihilate all the
state governments, and reduce this country to one single government."[29] Further, they complained that nowhere in the Constitution were there "measures to insure the independence and
vigor of the states."[30] As Storing points out, they objected to the
absence of any explicit reservations on behalf of the states; they
complained that the central authority's ability to call up militia
transformed those state forces into instruments of the national
authority and deprived the states of the most basic attribute of
sovereignty—control over the legitimate use of force; and they
claimed that the Senate did not really institutionalize the states
qua states because senators would vote as individuals, not as
delegates of the states. The states' power to appoint meant little
without the power to control or dismiss.

Under the proposed Constitution, the states would have virtually no role in the operation of the national authority. What
role they would have in the regime is confined to the residue of
power they retain—but it is the national government that would
police the boundaries between national and state authorities. "It
is true," Madison wrote, "that in controversies relating to the
boundary between the two jurisdictions, the tribunal which is ultimately to decide, is to be established under the general government. But this does not change the principle of the case."[31] The
Anti-Federalists saw this for the sophistry that it was. Indeed,
in another well-known paper on separation of powers, Madison
himself frankly reported that "mere parchment distinctions" are
insufficient to maintain boundaries of power. He did not apply
this insight to the issue of federalism. The structural properties of
the regime are much more determinative of real power than the
nominal allocations of power, and, correctly, the Anti-Federalists

saw precious little *structural* support for states in the Constitution. If the national government decided what was "national" and what was of local or state concern, "federalism" was transformed from a constitutive feature of the Constitution to a matter of discretionary national policy.

This last point is the key one and, in fact, *The Federalist* follows its rhetorical gestures to mollify skeptics with a sophisticated version of these Anti-Federalist objections. The "federal" or state-oriented features of the Constitution are not core or constitutive aspects—they are peripheral to a regime whose animating logic is national. Nonetheless, they are not mere tactical concessions. They help to make a better national, but not federal, regime. The criticisms of centralized authority and the virtues of localism are often sensible cautions about the harmful effects on political life of a large administrative state. Policies may sometimes be better executed or even perhaps better formulated at the state or local level than at the national level. The Constitution transforms this fact from one of invariable constitutional principle to one of discretionary national policy. That is, the national legislature may wisely leave matters to states or decentralize the administration of policy, but it is a national standard, a national assessment, that is the basis of such devolution and it might vary as circumstances vary.

Early in *The Federalist*, Hamilton sought to reassure voters that states would retain authority because they would remain the level of government to which the people would be most attached and therefore possessed of greater political legitimacy than the national level. It is worth quoting this reassurance at length:

> There is one transcendent advantage belonging to the province of the State governments, which alone suffices to place the matter in a clear and satisfactory light—I mean the ordinary administration of criminal and civil justice. This, of all others, is the most powerful, most universal, and most attractive source of popular obedience and attachment. It is this which, being the immediate and visible guardian of life and property, having its benefits and its terrors in constant activity before the public eye, regulating all those personal interests

and familiar concerns to which the sensibility of individuals is more immediately awake, contributes more than any other circumstance to impressing upon the minds of the people affection, esteem, and reverence towards the government. This great cement of society, which will diffuse itself almost wholly through the channels of the particular governments, independent of all other causes of influence, would insure them so decided an empire over their respective citizens as to render them at all times a complete counterpoise, and, not infrequently, dangerous rivals to the power of the Union.

The operations of the national government, on the other hand, falling less immediately under the observation of the mass of the citizens, the benefits derived from it will chiefly be perceived and attended to by speculative men. Relating to more general interests, they will be less apt to come home to the feelings of the people; and, in proportion, less likely to inspire an habitual sense of obligation and an active sentiment of attachment.[32]

Hamilton opened this theme, midway through *Federalist* No. 17, with what seemed to be a throwaway line that hinted that this elaborate account was a rhetorical gesture to partisans of the states and that his subsequent argument would point in the opposite direction. Hamilton said "each State would be apt to feel a stronger bias toward their local governments than toward the Union; *unless the force of that principle should be destroyed by a much better administration of the latter*"[33] (italics ours). Much of the later argument of *The Federalist* is devoted to showing that the true advantage of the Constitution and of national authority within it would be its better administration. Indeed, in *Federalist* No. 27, Hamilton states "there is a probability that the general government will be better administered than the states." Moreover, he continued, as the authority of the national government expanded and its effects penetrated the daily lives of ordinary citizens, its legitimacy would be further enhanced over the states.

I will, in this place, hazard an observation which will not be the less just because to some it may appear new; which is, that the more the operations of the national authority are intermingled in the ordinary exercise of government, the more the citizens are accustomed to meet with it in the common occurrences of their political life, the more it is familiarized to the sight and to their feelings, the further it enters into those objects which touch the most sensible chords and put in motion the most active springs of the human heart, the greater will be the probability that it will conciliate the respect and attachment of the community.[34]

Why would the national government be so visible in day-to-day political life if the most important tasks of government other than national defense—police powers, regulation, domestic welfare, and so forth—are reserved to the states? As with the issue of where legitimacy and attachment would lodge, *The Federalist* shifts from a mollifying rhetoric of deference to state sovereignty to a sophisticated version of the Anti-Federalists' animating observation that the national government would over time supplant the states.

The Federalists' rhetorical sophistication emerges as they stress the virtues of the very thing that they had previously said would be unlikely. In a point that has taken solid root in American political culture ever since, *The Federalist* reassured the Anti-Federalists that the national government was given only powers enumerated in the Constitution, with all other powers reserved to the states: the national government would be confined to those enumerated powers. The Anti-Federalists argued that the specific powers granted (especially taxation and commerce), along with the Necessary and Proper and Supremacy clauses, meant that over time the national government would usurp state authority and relegate states to total dependency on the national government. After insisting that the national government would possess only enumerated powers, Hamilton expanded and justified the Anti-Federalist insight about the logic of the Constitution. The Anti-Federalists had proposed cutting back on powers that might be abused in order to make those powers safe. Hamilton's reply is that it makes no sense to deny any competent authority all the power necessary to accomplish its legitimate purposes. "Limited government," then, should refer to the *purposes* of power, not the amount of power required to effect legitimate purposes. Although any power that can be used for good purposes might also be abused, Hamilton argued, it makes better sense to control potential abuse by making power accountable or by contesting its exercise with some competing powers in competing institutions than to deny the government the capacity to do what is necessary to accomplish its legitimate purposes:

> This is one of those truths which to a correct and unprejudiced mind carries its own evidence along with it, and may be obscured, but cannot be made plainer by argument or reasoning. It rests on axioms as simple as they are universal; the *means* ought to be proportioned to the *end*; the persons from whose agency the attainment of any *end* is expected ought to possess the means by which it is to be attained.[35]

Hamilton thus argued that the "necessary and proper" clause simply made clear the logic inherent in the granting of the primary powers in the first place. "These powers ought to exist without limitation" because one can't foresee all the circumstances for which they will be necessary. This logic suggests that over time circumstances that were initially "local" and beyond the scope of federal authority might, in different circumstance (perhaps changed socioeconomic conditions facilitated by the Constitution itself), become "national." Thus as the nation's economy became more complex and robust, the power to regulate commerce might similarly expand. Indeed, in a subsequent iteration of the syllogism quoted above, Hamilton slips in another proposition that makes problematic the whole idea of "limited government." In *Federalist* No. 31, Hamilton again begins with an assertion of the self-evidence of first principles and lists several maxims in ethics and politics:

> that there cannot be an effect without a cause; that the means ought to be proportioned to the end; that every power ought to be commensurate with its object; that there ought to be no limitation of a power destined to effect a purpose *which is itself incapable of limitation.*[36] (italics ours)

With these rhetorical iterations, Hamilton brings the reader to see that the subject of the Anti-Federalist complaint about the

Constitution is an ineluctable fact or necessity of a well-designed political order. If power needs to be unlimited to effect legitimate purposes, and if those purposes themselves can expand over time, how is limited government possible? Against the Anti-Federalist argument that the Constitution be abandoned or modified to cut back on national power, *The Federalist* defends the Constitution's novel solution to this problem—that power be cabined principally by structural provisions that create competing sources of power. In this way, *The Federalist* moves beyond its temporary concession that federalism is the problem to be solved and "new federalism" is the constitutional solution to a deeper claim, that the core organization issue for the Constitution is separation of powers, not federalism.

This sophisticated shift in argument from federalism to separation of powers as the key to the constitutional architecture has been largely lost in American political culture as a result of Anti-Federal interventions. Thomas Jefferson began a long tradition of Anti-Federal appropriation of Federalist rhetoric for the purpose of subversion because he failed, or refused, to recognize and endorse the shift that *The Federalist* made. "The capital and leading object of the constitution," Jefferson wrote in a letter to Justice William Johnson in 1823, "was to leave with the States all authorities which respected their own citizens only and to transfer to the United States those which respected citizens of foreign or other States, to make us several as to ourselves but one as to all others."[37] Through the weight of his political stature and praise of *The Federalist*, Jefferson deflected attention from the shift and helped to turn the Anti-Federal movement against the Constitution into a states' rights tradition within American political culture.[38]

If Jefferson lent authority to *The Federalist*, while reinterpreting its message, James Madison further complicated the picture and helped to entrench the success of the appropriation by Anti-Federalists and their heirs. Although he led the fight against the Anti-Federalists during the drafting and ratification of the Constitution and in the drafting of the Bill of Rights in the First

Congress, Madison later joined the cause of Republican heirs of the Anti-Federalists led by Thomas Jefferson. Political theorists have failed to satisfactorily reconcile the two conflicting sides of Madison's career, but for us, Madison's post-ratification alliance with Jefferson helps to explain the success of the Anti-Federal appropriation. The later Madison can be invoked as authority for Anti-Federal appropriations of *The Federalist*'s Madison.

SEPARATION OF POWERS

Returning to Publius, James Madison in *The Federalist*, the solution to the potential abuse of power was not to be found in limiting the national power necessary to accomplish national purposes and bolstering the authority of states; it would be accomplished by arranging structures of the central government to house overlapping and competing powers. The result was a new form of democratic governance—one could call it "mixed democracy" in which the desiderata of democracy itself were embedded in institutions designed to vindicate their competing perspectives on the democratic political project. The Constitution does not set up a structure like those of older mixed regimes in which contending claims to rule and competing social orders (monarchy, aristocracy, and democracy) were represented in distinct institutions such as the executive and the upper and lower houses of the legislature; instead it creates institutions that represent different aspects of democracy—institutionalizing the tension between such democratic qualities as popular will or majority will and protection of individual rights. *The Federalist* shifts the discussion from powers to the structures that house powers and the ways those structures would operate.

It is hard to imagine today, but in late eighteenth-century America, the politically attentive public—people who read newspaper columns like those that became *The Federalist*—were familiar with the political theory of Montesquieu, or at least with his principle that legislative, executive, and judicial power should be separated and confined to different departments of government. Reflecting on the ratification debate, Madison said to his colleagues in the First Congress that no argument had been urged with more success than the charge that the Constitution violated separation of powers.[39] In the proposed Constitution, the Senate shared appointment and treaty-making power with the executive, the executive held a qualified veto over legislation, and the judiciary had assigned powers sufficient to justify review of the constitutionality of legislation. Legislative, executive, and judicial powers were commingled in the Constitution in these and other ways contrary to Montesquieu's principle of separation.

Seizing on these facts, Anti-Federalists pressed their case to reject the proposed redesign of the governmental order. They argued that the separation of powers principle was an essential protection for liberty—a bulwark against tyranny; that assigning powers cleanly to the appropriate institutions facilitated efficiency in governance; conversely, that sharing power would generate too much conflict among the branches; and that the complexity of an arrangement of shared powers made government less comprehensible to ordinary citizens and therefore less accountable. As Bernard Manin states, "The Anti-Federalists unremittingly advocated precision and certainty in constitutional matters. They complained over and over again that the constitution was 'incomprehensible and indefinite,' 'vague and inexplicit.'"[40]

The Federalist responded to this complaint in a series of papers (*Federalist* Nos. 47–50) in which it is argued that like the issue of federalism, what was being proposed was not something fundamentally new but rather an improved version of what was already familiar. Here, though, Madison began by claiming that Anti-Federalists had mischaracterized prevailing theory and practice. Madison argued that the "oracle" Montesquieu did not separate power as cleanly as the purported idea of the separation of powers suggests—and that he indeed endorsed the idea that there be "partial agency" or sharing of the respective powers. Tyranny results, in this view, not from sharing per se, but rather from one branch possessing the whole of two sorts of power (for example, both legislative and executive power). Further, the state governments already shared power in their constitutions. Separation was not so clearly demarcated in the existing state governments. The "checks and balances" aspect of separation of powers is revealed to be a feature of already known theory and practice.

However, in *Federalist* No. 48, Madison begins to pivot and his next iteration of the argument proves, again, to be a sophisticated version of the Anti-Federalist understanding. Madison now criticized those very same state governments for being too attached to a naïve view of separation of powers, one that does not pay sufficient attention to the structural mechanisms necessary to maintain the separations. The state governments are faulted for relying too heavily on just the sort of separation of powers idea he said they did not rely upon—"parchment distinctions." Here is where *The Federalist* makes its now famous claim that "a mere demarcation on parchment of the constitutional limits of the several departments is not a sufficient guard against those encroachments which lead to a tyrannical concentration of all the powers of government in the same hands."[41]

Many of the state constitutions included the separation of powers principle as an explicit clause. There is no separation of powers clause in the American Constitution. Why not? Madison shows why the separation of powers idea needs to be jettisoned. Discussing the task of a constitutional designer, he mentions that the political architect needs to discern the natures of the different powers and assign them to the appropriate institutions. But there is no account of the nature of power in *The Federalist*. Rather, Madison describes the difficulty, perhaps impossibility, of characterizing powers by their natures:

> When we pass from the works of nature, in which all the delineations are perfectly accurate and appear to be otherwise only from the imperfection of the eye which surveys them, to the institutions of man, in which the obscurity arises as well from the object itself as from the organ by which it is contemplated, we must perceive the necessity of moderating still further our expectations and hopes for the efforts of human sagacity. Experience has instructed us that no skill in the science of government has yet been able to discriminate and define with sufficient certainty, its three great provinces—the

legislative, executive and judiciary; or even the privileges and powers of the different legislative branches. Questions daily occur in the course of practice which prove the obscurity which reigns in these subjects, and which puzzle the greatest adepts in political science.[42]

The well-known argument regarding separation of powers, from *Federalist* Nos. 47–51, turns out to be the preface or introduction to a new, complex governmental form for which there are no known precedents and no new label. Madison retains the old label, separation of powers, while changing its meaning. This new form we call "mixed democracy," as shorthand for an arrangement in which different institutions are constructed to vindicate and defend different democratic perspectives (popular will, individual rights, and so on). Power or functional powers still play an important role in this new system but now subordinate to different structures designed to induce different ways of seeing the same policy choices. *The Federalist* shifts the core idea of constitutional design from one in which powers are the main characters and structures play a supporting role to the reverse— with structure the main issue and powers the secondary point. Because *The Federalist* continued to describe this new system as a "separation of powers" system, that terminology has allowed some heirs of the Anti-Federalists to resurrect the abandoned separation of powers idea in court doctrine and in American political rhetoric even though both the Anti-Federalists (explicitly) and the Federalists (more subtly) indicated that the Constitution itself does not fully embrace that older notion.

Federalist rhetoric on separation of powers displays a similar pattern to that which we sketched with respect to federalism. In both, *The Federalist* makes a series of arguments—early iterations reassuring concerned citizens that the change is not what the Anti-Federalists describe, followed by a sophisticated version of the Anti-Federalist picture.

Federalism and separation of powers are the two great topics and sources of dispute in the ratification debate. The pattern of rhetorical iteration in *The Federalist* and later appropriation by Anti-Federalists is replicated in subsidiary topics as well, including the likelihood of a standing army, the alleged monarchical character of the presidency, and the extraordinary scope of judicial power.

The Anti-Federalists feared that standing armies—a professional military supported in times of peace as well as war—would replace temporary citizen militias as the main means of national defense. They pointed out that the Constitution did not proscribe standing armies in peacetime and indeed created a regime that would be likely to raise a standing army in the future. The prospect of immense power at the disposal of a potentially tyrannical central government or controlled by a strong president, along with a worry that standing armies might change the very character of a republican polity, resonated well enough with uncertain citizens that *The Federalist* devoted five papers to the subject. Initially, in *Federalist* No. 8, Hamilton concedes the worry—that it would be a serious problem to support a standing army in times of peace as well as war—but argues that the Constitution offers better protection against this possibility than would dissolution of the confederation into separate competing states. However, in subsequent papers 24, 25, and 26 by Hamilton, and 41 by Madison, *The Federalist* lays out a picture of a future world that might well require standing armies and lauds the Constitution's provision for this possibility. As Madison explained:

> But was it necessary to give an INDEFINITE POWER of raising TROOPS, as well as providing fleets; and of maintaining both in PEACE as well as in War? . . . How could a readiness for war in time of peace be safely prohibited, unless we could prohibit in like manner the preparations and establishments of every hostile nation? The means of security can only be regulated by the means and danger of attack.[43]

When Anti-Federalists complained that the presidency would effectively be a monarchy, *The Federalist* first denied the charge, pointing out that titles of nobility are proscribed in the new Constitution. But *The Federalist* then defended "energy" in the executive—appropriating the power of monarchs for republican purposes.[44] When the Anti-Federalists argued that eliminating inheritance as a basis of rule would still allow a monarchy, albeit an elective one, *The Federalist* responded in a way that endorses the Anti-Federal, and then-conventional, understanding that accountability to republican principles requires virtue in its officeholders. "It will not be too strong to say that there will be a constant probability of seeing the station filled by characters pre-eminent for ability and virtue," Hamilton says in *Federalist* No. 68. As had been the pattern, that mollification is not the last word. In *Federalist* No. 76, Hamilton revised: "there will always be great probability of having the place [of the presidency] supplied by a man of abilities, at least respectable." Virtue as a protection for liberty is replaced by the agonistic contestation of institutions based on contending democratic principles in a truly new constitution—one that departed from known forms and tested practices, just as the Anti-Federalists had charged.

Finally, when the brilliant Anti-Federalist "Brutus" presents a compelling picture of the development of the Supreme Court over time, showing how its structure and powers portend an institution that will make broad policy decisions under the guise of legal interpretation, *The Federalist* responds, initially, that the judiciary is the "least dangerous branch," and then shifts to a case for a strong power of judicial review of the constitutionality of legislation.[45]

On every contested topic, *The Federalist*'s rhetorical strategy is to follow an initial denial of the logic of the Anti-Federalist position with a second or third iteration in which the normative conclusion of the Anti-Federalist is contested but the Anti-Federal picture of the logic of American political development is elaborated and endorsed. This rhetorical strategy helped Federalists succeed in the ratification debate, yet it provided the tools and authority by which their constitutional intentions and aspirations could, to this day, be challenged.

Heirs to the Anti-Federalists

As a result of (1) Anti-Federalists' provocation, (2) *The Federalist*'s iterative response, and (3) the subsequent strategic appropriation of *Federalist* rhetoric by Anti-Federalists and their heirs, the Anti-Federalists maintain a remarkable hold on American politics. Yet this influence is generally unappreciated. Many, perhaps most, of the followers of the Anti-Federalists are unwitting. They imagine themselves to be followers of the Federalists or of the "founders" of the American Constitution when they, in fact, advocate positions and understandings directly counter to those of the actual Federalists. The Constitution continues to operate according to a political logic of national development about which there was remarkable agreement between Federalists and Anti-Federalists at the Founding. However, overlaid on top of its political logic are misunderstandings generated by the art of appropriation that we have described. Because these misunderstandings have taken root in American political culture, they have themselves become operative features of modern American politics. One need look no further than the 2016 presidential contest. With the death of Supreme Court Justice Antonin Scalia, pundits, supporters, and detractors alike eulogized him with references to his commitment to "originalism," and the Republican candidates immediately introduced into their campaigns claims about who among them was best suited to appoint a "constitutionalist" like Scalia, worthy of his seat. At the outset of this chapter we noted that Scalia himself misunderstood *The Federalist* in his Affordable Care Act dissent, and his conservative brethren appear to be magnifying this mistake in their commemorations of him.

This practice of mistaken attribution is commonplace. In the subsequent two chapters of this book, we show how the mechanism of *Federalist* appropriation exploited by the losers of the Founding of the Constitution is amplified by additional strategies developed by the political losers of the Reconstruction contest (Andrew Johnson) and of the New Deal (Barry Goldwater). Their actions contributed to the solidification of misattribution. Yet they are not the only ones who were influenced by the Anti-Federal success. In the remaining pages of this chapter, we offer some general remarks about the political actors who, unwittingly or not, have misattributed Anti-Federal claims to the Federalists, and here we focus largely on contemporary political attributions. When considered alongside the regime antimoments described in the next two chapters, these varied additional examples illuminate how the Anti-Federal appropriation undergirds—and helps to explain—the power of the conservative tradition in American political development.

Because we seek to add a new perspective and new evidence to what is already known about the key junctures in American political development, this book focuses on the conservative tradition as it marked the losing side of each of the major constitutional crises. However, it would be wrong to conclude that only conservatives on the right have been heirs to the Anti-Federalists. As we suggest here and again in the next chapter, progressives on the left also evidence the unnoticed long-term victory of the Founding's losers.

While the distortions of *The Federalist* and of the political logic of the Constitution that it defends can be found in the writings and speeches of partisans on all sides of the political spectrum, there is a pattern to these Anti-Federal appropriations. Conservatives usually urge an Anti-Federal understanding of federalism, whereas progressives are split on this point. Some progressives see and embrace the Hamiltonian logic that tied expanding power to meet expanding national exigencies and purposes, while others accept the Anti-Federal understanding of the Constitution as a charter for only limited national power and urge that it be updated, replaced, or reinterpreted as a "living document." Progressives often express an Anti-Federal posture on separation of powers, especially when the presidency is held by an opposing party. Conservatives are split on this point with some, like Justice Scalia, embracing a Hamiltonian understanding of executive power and others, like Libertarian Rand Paul, expressing the Anti-Federal perspective.

The progressive misunderstanding of the political logic of the Constitution began with Woodrow Wilson. Wilson argued that the Constitution was inadequate to the demands of twentieth-century governance. In making a case for democratizing the presidency, he described the defects of the separation of powers system in ways that echoed the initial and disingenuous Federalist response to the Anti-Federalists and appeared oblivious to their later more sophisticated account.

Wilson thought that the Constitution's form of separated powers reflected the Federalists' "enthusiasm" for Montesquieu and also their Newtonian inclinations ("They constructed a government as they would have constructed an orrery,—to display the laws of nature").[46] Both of these characterizations missed or ignored Madison's arguments that the Constitution improved upon, and departed from, Montesquieu and his view that the artifices of government cannot clearly conform to nature, points we stressed earlier. The Federalists' expectation for "mixed democracy" along with their expectation that power needed to be commensurate with national purposes was far more compatible with Wilson's own political objectives than he himself realized. In this sense, early twentieth-century progressivism was not as much a reaction against the limits of the Constitution—as it is commonly understood and as progressives themselves understood their task—as it was an elaboration and endorsement of the path that both Anti-Federalists and Federalists anticipated, the former with dread and the latter with hope. And in misunderstanding the constitutional sources of the trajectory that progressivism enacted, they wedded an Anti-Federal induced misunderstanding to a Federalist project. Some of the dilemmas that attend American governance today reflect that uneasy conjunction.[47]

While modern proponents of enhanced national government power, including Woodrow Wilson and, more famously, Franklin Roosevelt, were advocating policies in line with the sophisticated Federalist argument about federalism as well as with "mixed democracy," the nationalist programs of these progressives are widely thought to be pressing against constitutional limits. Accepting the appropriated rendering of *The Federalist*'s Constitution to be a static division of state and national power, some supporters of these progressives thought the original Constitution inadequate to address the national problems generated by modern social and economic change and argued for the need to revise, or even abandon, the Constitution.[48]

At the very same time, opponents of New Deal legislation, including such core legislative achievements as the Social Security Act, often claimed that the power accorded to the national government by the legislation was contrary to what "the framers of the Constitution ever contemplated"[49]—again revealing the appropriation of the rhetoric of the Constitution's advocates by Anti-Federalists and their heirs intent on counteracting the polity's political and constitutional logic.

It is important to stress that we are not assessing or endorsing the merits of progressive and Democratic initiatives. Nor do we mean to suggest that the Federalists would have endorsed every New Deal initiative. Our concern is not with the merits of the policies but with the character and source of the arguments made by proponents and opponents alike. Both the proponents' claim that the Constitution did not provide for a strong national government and the opponents' claim that the policies were unconstitutional follow from the post-ratification appropriation of early *Federalist* arguments by Anti-Federalists and their heirs and underscore how successful Anti-Federalists were in ultimately dominating constitutional discourse around federalism.

As we show in chapter 4, modern conservative politicians like Barry Goldwater continue to return to early iterations of the Federalist argument to justify positions on states' rights. In contemporary constitutional discourse, conservative justices and constitutional interpreters often cite the "original intent" of the framers to make limited national government and robust state sovereignty a core concern of the Constitution. For example, according to legal scholar H. Jefferson Powell, Supreme Court Justice William Rehnquist rooted his conservative theory of federalism in the framers' intent. As Powell notes, in doing so, Rehnquist "seems to have fallen into the curious historical error of projecting the language and thought of the *opponents* of the Constitution onto its drafters." Rehnquist's federalism "far from being 'the intention of the Framers,' is an inadvertent repudiation of part of their achievement."[50]

The hero of the contemporary Republican Party, Ronald Reagan, was also famous for proselytizing the view that it was the framers' intent to limit national government power in favor of a governmental system that was a "federation of sovereign states."[51] His political career is literally bookended by this rhetoric. In his 1964 speech nominating Goldwater for the Republican presidential candidacy, "A Time for Choosing," Reagan claimed, "'the full power of centralized government'—this was the very thing the Founding Fathers sought to minimize." And in his final presidential State of the Union Address in 1988, Reagan continued to argue, "We're for limited government because we understand, as the Founding Fathers did, that it is the best way of ensuring personal liberty and empowering the individual." In making an argument about limited government as equal to state sovereignty, Reagan sometimes directly referenced the authority of *The Federalist*: "While much of the 20th century saw the rise of the Federal Government, the 21st century will be the century of the States. I have always believed that America is strongest and freest and happiest when it is truest to the wisdom of its founders. In *Federalist* No. 45, James Madison wrote that 'The powers delegated by the Constitution to the Federal Government are few and defined. Those which are to remain in the State Government are numerous and indefinite.' Or to put it another way, 'We the People.'"[52] In what has become a common habit of the modern intellectual heirs of the Anti-Federalists, Reagan appropriates the early, defensive rhetoric of *The Federalist* to make a constitutional claim that advances the Anti-Federal project.

Given that such leading lights of modern conservatism as Scalia, Rehnquist, and Reagan have rooted their philosophy of federalism in the framers' early and disingenuous rhetoric, is it any wonder that today's political actors and activists do the same? For this error of associating a primary emphasis on a state sovereignty definition of limited government with the Constitution's creators continues to amplify through the rhetoric of contemporary Republican politics. Citing limited government as among the essential "principles that guide us," eventual 2012 Republican vice presidential nominee Paul Ryan described the idea as "anchored in the wisdom of the founders."[53] In making his, ultimately unsuccessful, case for the 2012 Republican presidential nomination, Newt Gingrich argued that the "Founding Fathers" fought for "local power" and "smaller, more effective, limited government"[54] and ultimately created a government that "was *not* authorized to become the producer and director of the great drama that is America."[55] Sarah Palin, the 2008 Republican vice presidential nominee, argued that the "way forward" was to "devolve powers back locally where the Founders intended them to be."[56] Another 2012 presidential hopeful, Ron Paul, claimed, "The Founders assured that the individual states would be responsible for protection of their own citizens and their goal was strictly to restrain the federal government in any abuse of our liberties."[57]

Similar mistakes are made by conservative activists on the ground, including those associated with the contemporary Tea Party, who claim that a close reading of the Constitution and the Declaration of Independence justifies their ideological and policy positions. That the framers' priority was to limit national government power is an article of faith among contemporary Tea Party activists and is espoused by their congressional political representatives as well. As Theda Skocpol and Vanessa Williamson write in their study of modern Tea Partiers:

> Despite their fondness for the Founding Fathers, Tea Party members we met did not make any reference to the intellectual battles and political compromises out of which the Constitution and its subsequent amendments were forged. . . . Nor did they realize the extent to which some of the positions Tea Partiers now espouse bear a close resemblance to those of the Anti-Federalists—the folks the Founders were countering in their effort to establish sufficient federal authority to ensure a truly *United* States. The Tea Parties we met did not show any awareness that they are echoing arguments made by the Nullifiers and Secessionists before and during the U.S. Civil

War, or that their stress on "states' rights" is eerily reminiscent of dead-ender white opposition to Civil Rights laws in the 1960s.[58]

It is important to stress that the issues at stake here are the misunderstandings of the logic of the Constitution and the authority of the framers. Although they are mistaken in their invocations of authority, some of these positions may be reasonable criticisms of contemporary public policy. For example, it may be wise for the Congress to decentralize some programs or to devolve some responsibilities to states or localities. The misunderstandings do not go to the merits of particular national policy decisions but rather to the claims that the national government does not have responsibility for national problems or that the state governments may ignore national claims to authority.[59] The heirs of the Anti-Federalists may also have viable and important criticisms of the constitutional order and its logic of development. It may well be the case, for example, that government is just too big or that the national government is just too strong as the Anti-Federalists feared it would become. However, if true, such claims would imply the need for a new constitution rather than a more faithful recovery and restoration of the one we have purportedly abandoned.

A Hybrid Political Order

The Anti-Federalists lost the political war over ratification of the Constitution in 1788, but they and their heirs have won many subsequent battles regarding the interpretation of the Constitution in practice. The result has been a hybrid political order: the political logic of the Constitution has unfolded and operated as both the Anti-Federalists and Federalists suggested it would, yet, at the same time, that unfolding logic has been regarded as a departure from the Constitution. It is seen as a departure on account of the rhetorical sleight of hand that Federalists had to proffer in order to overcome resistance to ratification. Looking back on the founding debate, this is a substantial and long-term

Anti-Federal victory, amazing to behold. By using the defensive rhetoric of that authoritative source, *The Federalist*, as ammunition against the Anti-Federalists' own best understanding of the consequences of adopting the Constitution, Anti-Federalist heirs created space for an interpretation of the Constitution that subverts its animating logic. *The Federalist* provided the rhetorical resources that enabled their opposition to regroup and attempt to achieve through interpretation what they could not achieve in the original constitutional construction.

The recent partisan debate regarding Medicare illustrates how the constitutional order operates as a hybrid—its original logic still in play but under siege at the very same time. Recall that Hamilton indicated that good administration would bind the citizenry to the centralized government despite its distance. Modern heirs to the Anti-Federalists suggest that governmental centralization of medical care (such as Obamacare) is contrary to the Constitution; at the same time they criticize any innovation that would "take away" or cut back an existing program of centralized medical provision, such as Medicare. To understand these contradictory propositions, we must turn to the hybridity of the constitutional order bequeathed to America. These same modern Anti-Federalists *were* opposed to Medicare when the program was initially proposed, and now they oppose any governmental alternative to it because the Constitution worked according to the logic that the original Anti-Federalists feared and that Hamilton defended. American politics can be understood as a layered political development, vibrant Anti-Federal ideas layered over and in tension with the unfolding Federalist design. We return to this theme in our concluding chapter.

Reconstruction
Andrew Johnson's Politics
of Obstruction

Andrew Johnson is generally regarded as one of the worst presidents in American political history. It would be hard to think of a clearer example of failed leadership. His vision and his specific plans for bringing the South back into the Union were rejected by Congress. He aggressively opposed the major post–Civil War Reconstruction agenda, which was legislated by Northerners in Congress over his vetoes. Amendments to the Constitution that he opposed were passed by Congress and ratified by a northern national majority. The victorious opposition against him included leaders of Johnson's own governing coalition, and they grew to detest him. Johnson's extraordinary string of political defeats culminated in his impeachment, the first of a president. He escaped conviction by the narrowest of margins and left office politically defeated and disgraced.

Yet it was Andrew Johnson's vision, not that of Reconstruction lawmakers, that reconstituted American politics. Despite the significance of the "second American founding," policies similar to those Johnson had advanced as president quickly replaced those that constituted the Reconstruction agenda, evidencing such a powerful hold on the polity that they made a mockery of the amended Constitution. Johnson's vision was woven into the very fabric of American political life for a century, in ways that we still contend with today. Less than a handful of presidents have been as successful as Andrew Johnson in advancing their political project.[1]

That Andrew Johnson failed to legislate his vision while in office and that American political development subsequently came to be characterized by policies close to those he preferred are facts that would be difficult to contest. Indeed, while Anti-Federal success in influencing constitutional interpretation is not very well appreciated, the failure to adhere to post–Civil War Reconstruction amendments in any meaningful fashion is well known. It is therefore surprising that major studies of American politics that conjoin Andrew Johnson's legislative defeats and eventual policy success are so difficult to find. Perhaps this reflects social science's discomfort with the ironic. Our central argument, however, goes beyond reflection on the ironic conjunction. We claim that these two facts are connected historically, that Andrew Johnson's political failure as a president was itself the instrument for the later success of his policies.

In this chapter, we muster substantial evidence that Johnson's actions—his rhetoric as well as his executive and political decisions—*facilitated* the establishment of policies that bore the stamp of his vision. Southern elites in the nineteenth century, witnessing Johnson's leadership, anticipated his legacy. In the aftermath of the Civil War, for example, most southern elites believed that only the right to secession and slavery had been lost, not the rights to manage race and class relations as they saw fit. Former Confederate leaders, including Jefferson Davis, prophesied that the "Southern cause" would find new form and a new time. And as southern historian Edward Pollard, writing contemporaneously, described, Andrew Johnson was just the man for that job. In *The Lost Cause* (1866), Pollard wrote that Johnson "saw before him a part in American history second only to that of George Washington; he left behind him the ambitions and resentments of mere party; he rose as the man who has been secretly, almost unconsciously, great. . . . The man who had been twitted as a tailor and condemned as a demagogue, proved a statesman, measuring his actions for the future, insensible to clamour and patient for results."[2] Pollard saw in his fellow Southerner, President Johnson, a "patient" and "great" leader, a "statesman." This was, of course, not how most Northerners at the time, especially Radical Republicans, saw him. Nor is it how he is generally remembered in the historical record, despite the recognition that his political vision prevailed. Our best evidence of his role in facilitating his preferred changes, however, comes from an interpretation of Johnson's actions themselves, from the logic and character of his distinctive brand of leadership. When one looks anew at Johnson's political "failures," one can see that their meaning and effects extended well beyond the Washington community to incipient coalitions in the nation at large and especially among the defeated elites of the South.

When he assumed the presidency after Lincoln's assassination, Andrew Johnson adopted a style of leadership that is hard to understand in conventional terms. As leader of the Union's governing party, Johnson was in a position to use his inherited authority to seize on efforts by the congressional leadership to reach an accommodation with him regarding the shape of Reconstruction. The record of the period is replete with opportunities (some of which we describe later) for Johnson to very substantially moderate the Radical Republican agenda and to reintegrate the South into the Union on terms that at the time would have been satisfactory to many in that region and consistent with the core principles of the Republican Party of which he was the purported leader. Instead, Johnson chose to advance a program contrary to the core principles of the coalition he inherited from Lincoln, and he attempted to block every major policy initiative for Reconstruction that would have been supported by a large Union coalition. We describe this leadership style as preemptive and obstructionist.

Because preemption and obstruction were so unsuccessful during Johnson's term in office, and because more conventional approaches would have won him legislative accomplishment and perhaps even election to the office he inherited, one might conclude that Johnson was mentally deranged, or at least politically tone-deaf. His failures and that characterization call to mind Woodrow Wilson's obdurate fight for a League of Nations.[3] But, like Wilson's defeat, Johnson's political tactics were more rational than conventional accounts suggest. Johnson was a semiliterate man, not a sophisticated thinker like Wilson. Yet he developed an unusually powerful political sense while schooled on the stump in Tennessee. If he could not outline his political understanding for university press publication, he could feel it instinctively and act on it in the heat of political battle. (He was aided in this, of course, by the ready availability of the rhetorical resources bequeathed to him by earlier Anti-Federal heirs, as described in the previous chapter.) Johnson's political moves formed a remarkably coherent pattern, albeit one that reverses most conventional understandings of effective leadership.[4]

Johnson's politics of preemption and obstruction can be usefully categorized in two ways. First, Johnson used the resources of the executive office to rebuild the capacity of the South to politically engage the North on its own terms. He preempted Congress with his lenient "restoration plan" for the South and later willfully misexecuted the less forgiving plan of Congressional Reconstruction; these actions helped to bring about his impeachment, yet through them, Johnson provided the South with time to rebuild its social, economic, and, most important, civil infrastructure. Johnson also began to build new political coalitions and to link political allies outside the dominant party apparatus. The strategic subversions of "office" and "party" allowed southern elites the opportunity to regroup and to develop the networks necessary for reframing their political battle to preserve their racial-economic hierarchy. Second, Johnson disrupted the ideological frame that the politically and militarily successful Republican Party was intent on establishing. To the victor in politics typically goes the opportunity to establish the political narrative that will prevail. Because of the complex constitutional process by which Reconstruction Republicans were attempting to change the polity, Johnson was able to exploit the pulpit of the presidency to launch an alternative narrative of America and of constitutionality, often borrowing from Anti-Federalist discourse, now authoritative due to the heirs' appropriation from *The Federalist*, to do so. With this, he disrupted the Republicans' frame and constructed ideological space for the South to inhabit in defining the nation's political future. Each of these dimensions, capacity building and ideological construction, is considered in turn.

Capacity Building through Preemption and Obstruction

At the time of his assassination in 1865, President Lincoln had not yet committed himself to a particular path by which southern states were to be reincorporated into the Union. During the war, Lincoln was largely conciliatory. Lincoln's Ten Percent plan—which would have readmitted Louisiana, Tennessee, and Arkansas once 10 percent of voters eligible in 1860 (prior to the war) had taken an oath of loyalty and voted new state representation—would have excluded former slaves from political participation. His very choice of Andrew Johnson as his vice president, a southern Democrat who stayed loyal to the Union, is further evidence of his willingness to accommodate the South in hopes of a speedy restoration. Yet just prior to his death Lincoln was seriously considering a reintegration plan that would be more demanding, requiring, for example, at least limited African American suffrage. The upshot is that Johnson assumed the presidency without inheriting a clear plan of action from his predecessor.[5]

Radical Republicans in Congress and their supporters were initially optimistic that Johnson would impose an aggressive reconstruction plan on the South, largely owing to a misinterpretation of the intent behind some of his first comments after assuming the presidency (including, for example, his telling a group of Radical congressmen that "treason must be made infamous, and traitors must be impoverished"). Raised in poverty in the mountains of Tennessee, Johnson disliked the white planter elites who dominated southern politics before the war and who had led the rebellion. He had also recently been the target of an assassination attempt. The combination fueled his interest in punishing treason; it did not, as Radicals believed, extend to a principled commitment to Radical ideas.[6]

Radical Republicans were quickly disabused of their expectation. Johnson's first move was to institute a "restoration plan" for the South that was far more lenient than that desired by congressional Republicans. Reminiscent of Lincoln's assertion of executive authority at the outset of the Civil War, Johnson enacted his plan while Congress was in recess. Because the war was over, Johnson could easily have chosen to reconvene Congress for the purpose of establishing a jointly negotiated postwar agenda. He chose, instead, to preempt it. This decision to claim executive authority and preempt Congress was seen as a usurpation of power that was different from Lincoln's, precisely because hostilities between the states were over at the time of Johnson's action. And while Johnson cast his action as temporary, "the Southern States did not view the action of President Johnson as of a temporary character; on the contrary, it had the appearance of being, and it was treated as being, of a permanent character."[7] Thus, from the outset, states in the South understood Johnson's leadership for what it was: an effort to create for the region the political space to reincorporate on its own terms—not on the terms of the victorious North that Johnson was ostensibly leading—and expressly contrary to the conventional wisdom about the terms of war settlements that privilege the victor's demands.

The essence of Johnson's plan is contained in an Amnesty Proclamation and an accompanying program for the reintegration of North Carolina. Amnesty was to be granted to all who had participated in the rebellion if they took an oath of loyalty to the Union; the exceptions were former civil and military officers of the Confederacy and ex-Confederates who owned more than $20,000 worth of property. With amnesty came the restoration of all confiscated property except former slaves. The North Carolina Proclamation, subsequently extended to all other unreconstructed states, allowed loyal citizens (that is, those granted amnesty) who had been eligible to vote before the war to elect delegates to a convention at which a new state government would be formed and representatives to Congress chosen. The new state governments were obliged only to abolish slavery, repeal the secession ordinances, and repudiate their war debts.

Johnson's plan for "restoration" was lenient in that it enfranchised only white Southerners. It also did not redistribute land to former slaves or attend to their welfare, as would have been done by other policy proposals at the time.[8] Congressional Republicans, on the other hand, favored at least limited African American suffrage (ranging from moderate proposals to extend the vote to those who had served in the Union Army or were literate to radical proposals for universal manhood suffrage), and they advocated policies that would reconstruct southern civil society in a way that would make freedom for former slaves politically meaningful and economically viable. Johnson's proclamation would make eligibility for future electoral participation determined by individual states. This would, of course, leave the decision about black political rights in the hands of white Southerners. Additionally, in his Amnesty Proclamation, Johnson made available the possibility of individual pardons for those not included in the general amnesty. The president then proceeded to grant clemency to 13,500 out of 15,000 applicants, thus restoring citizenship and property rights to a large portion of the former Confederate elite.[9]

By preempting Congress with his restoration plan, Johnson strove to put the white South back on its political feet as quickly as possible. This would ensure that the region had the normal tools of political contestation, including congressional representation and some version of state sovereignty, with which to settle the terms of the postwar era. Short of the reinstitution of slavery, southern elites could not ask for better terms. Not only were

Johnson's conditions generous but the process of implementing them would be quick. Indeed, southern representatives were presenting themselves to be seated in Congress by the time that body reconvened in December 1865. True, the war effort in the South had cost $2.3 billion (far more than in the North, proportionate to resources), and repudiation of the debt left many without the opportunity to reclaim their former wealth. But the quicker they could restore their fields and resume economic production, the sooner they would return to prosperity.[10] Most important, as the South had been defeated militarily, a quick restoration of political representation in the national government was essential if white Southerners were to restrain (or reverse) policy initiatives of northern lawmakers. With a Democrat, albeit a Union loyalist, in the executive office, particularly one making overtures to the region, and sympathetic fellow Democrats still retaining a foothold in the North, a legislative remedy for some of the ills of defeat was entirely feasible.[11]

Johnson's preemptive move to quickly reinstate southern lawmakers was a clear act of legislative obstruction on the president's part, and Northerners knew it. As the editors of *Harper's Weekly* lamented in reflecting on Johnson's efforts:

Were the rebel States during hostilities, when their whole energies were concentrated into a public force and arrayed against the United States, entitled to be represented on the floor of Congress? No one will allege that they were. If they could not take part in Congress in determining how we should conduct the war against them, it follows that they can not take the same part in adjusting the terms of peace. These terms still remain to be arranged. This arrangement must be made upon the rule of international law, that, as one of the results of victory, the sovereignty of the United States immediately prevails over a conquered people. Any other idea would enable the Southern States, through means of representation in Congress or in local Legislatures, to obstruct such arrangements as are necessary to the safety of the Union. No other alternative would in that case remain but the further and interminable persecution of the war.[12]

Johnson's "victory" in peremptorily establishing his restoration plan led Northerners to quickly shed their initial hopefulness and organize an effort—successful at least in the short run—to thwart his agenda.[13]

By attempting to expedite the return of the southern states to the very national government against which they had just revolted, Johnson's plan gave the ambitions of the former Confederate elite not just new institutional footing but constitutional grounding as well. The premise on which Johnson developed his position was the supreme authority of the Founders' Constitution and the Union it created. Reflecting on his wartime loyalty to supporters in February 1866, Johnson said, "I said then that I was for the Union with slavery—or I was for the Union without slavery. In either alternative I was for my government and its Constitution."[14] It was this loyalty that had prevented him from joining his regional brethren in secession and motivated his denouncements of their treason. But because the Constitution provided no avenue by which states could withdraw from the Union, it was, in his logic, only traitorous individuals who had engaged in rebellion. Having quashed their efforts, the imperative was now on restoring to the loyal citizens residing in the South the republican form of government constitutionally promised to them. Since the war had been fought over secession and the supremacy of the constitutional order had been vindicated, all that was needed from the defeated was a renunciation of their efforts to withdraw and evidence of renewed loyalty to the Union; there was no reason to extract additional concessions, such as black suffrage. With the war question settled, the South should be free, according to Johnson, to return to the constitutional exercise of self-governance on its own terms.

In addition to returning the South to a role in national government, Johnson's plan recognized the integrity of the states and their sovereignty as decision makers. Entwined with his fealty to the Constitution were his beliefs in states' rights and white supremacy, products, in no small part, of his southern heritage as well as the influence of the Anti-Federal rhetorical appropriation.[15] His emphasis on the primacy of states as the locus for suffrage decisions and, more generally, in ordering affairs and protecting citizens was consistent with his (and the Anti-Federal heirs generally) reading of the Constitution. He had no interest in maintaining the strong centralized national government that had been so necessary to winning the war—he was a self-proclaimed "Jacksonian Democrat." While Johnson had eventually supported the abolition of slavery, his racism combined with his suspicion of federal dominion fortified his belief that the states should be left free to reconstruct their racial hierarchies on their own. For example, in replying to an African American delegation's request for black suffrage in 1866, Johnson said, "Each community is better prepared to determine the depository of its political power than anybody else, and it is for the legislature . . . to say who shall vote, and not the Congress of the United States."[16] That white Southerners, if given the opportunity, would prevent black enfranchisement was broadly evident and northern Reconstruction lawmakers pointed to this reality when making the case for national suffrage laws that aided blacks. Offering one such measure in 1869 (that would also have disenfranchised former white Confederate rebels), Samuel Shellabarger of Ohio argued, "Let it remain possible, under our amendment, to still disfranchise the body of the colored race in the late rebel States and I tell you it will be done. . . . The overwhelming and ocean-like volume of facts which comes to us every single day of our lives in undissenting voice proves that [southern whites] will submit to negro enfranchisement not an hour longer than compelled by Federal coercion, or as a necessity to reacquire admission to national power."[17] Thus, virtually every component of Johnson's restoration plan was designed to preemptively protect the former Confederacy from the congressional action of Northerners and to give the South the institutional and jurisdictional capacity to author its own rebuilding, including granting white Southerners their wish to prevent black suffrage.

Beyond official proclamations, Johnson promoted his goals through other unilateral actions, taking quick steps to restore to the South a proximate version of the antebellum economic and social order. Not only did he liberally pardon ex-Confederate leaders but he also directed that land confiscated by the Union Army be returned, rather than redistributed to former slaves, as leading Radicals such as Thaddeus Stevens wanted. He prioritized the use of civil government, particularly courts, over military government and tribunals, which had the effect of placing the old Confederate elite and their sympathizers in positions of civil and juridical authority. In defiance of a legislative act, Johnson refused to collect a levied cotton tax so as not to additionally burden economically struggling Southerners. To the extent possible, he removed black Union troops, and separately, he allowed for the organization of white southern militia to maintain order, in some cases overruling the orders of his own generals to do so.[18]

The president's actions created opportunities for the former rebels to assert control over the economic and racial reconstruction of their states, and they endowed the actions taken by local elites with legitimacy. For example, by insisting only on loyalty to the Union and by reinstating many former Confederate leaders, Johnson's restoration policy implicitly sanctioned the adoption of Black Codes, the state and local laws enacted to regulate the movement and employment of freedmen. By requiring blacks to carry written permission from employers to move about, imposing curfews, regulating social and civic gatherings, restricting access to certain trades, and outlawing "vagrancy," the Black Codes returned African Americans to virtual enslavement.[19] As one Republican touring the South at the time, put it, Black Codes made clear that "although the former owner has lost his individual property in the former slaves, the blacks at large belong to the whites at large."[20] While Johnson, given his childhood poverty, was no fan of the South's planter elite, the actions he pursued made them, and white Southerners more generally, clear beneficiaries of his agenda.

The Black Codes were the first articulation of the South's vision of a postslavery world, and congressional reaction to the readmittance of the states hardened in response to the enactment of the Codes. While the laws outraged many in the North and caused Johnson some political discomfort in Washington, they were nonetheless accommodated by his policy and by his strong "constitutional" defense of states' rights. Still less legitimate hallmarks of the Jim Crow South began to emerge at this time as well, most notably the reign of terror and violence by which whites enforced social, economic, and political domination of blacks. Riots, organized white militias, and the activities of the newly birthed Ku Klux Klan and similar organizations formed the informal police state that enforced white supremacy. Johnson's 1866 proclamation halting military tribunals and restoring civil court proceedings not only undermined military rule in the South but meant that many offenders faced sympathetic juries of white peers. Despite reports of escalating violence, Johnson did not back down from his stance, thus implicitly condoning the South's informal methods of state-controlled reconstruction. Johnson even went so far as to manipulate information on conditions in the South, most notably early in the promotion of his policy when he dispatched a more sympathetic General Grant to survey the South after receiving an unfavorable report by General Schurz.[21]

More than simply setting the agenda for postwar politics, Johnson's actions in this regard had the net effect of placing in the hands of the just-defeated rebels the tools for financial rebuilding; the means, including arms, for management of the social and racial order; and the sanctioning power of political authority. By facilitating the South's quick rejuvenation of its desired racial-economic order and civil infrastructure, Johnson's actions enabled his southern contemporaries to begin building the region's capacity for political engagement with the North on its own terms. Writing at the time, historian Pollard is again instructive. Pollard warned: "The people of the South have surrendered in the war what the war has conquered; but they cannot be expected to give up what was not involved in the war, and voluntarily abandon their political schools. . . . [A] 'war of ideas' is what the South wants and insists upon perpetrating."[22] As a region, the South had early adopted the strategic Anti-Federal appropriation of *The Federalist*, not in the least because it offered the surer defense of the region's interests. And in the aftermath of the Civil War, with the physical contest surrendered, the ambition to contest political outcomes through a "war of ideas" only intensified—giving the South an even greater stake in the Anti-Federal post-ratification tradition of constitutional interpretation. Significantly, Johnson signaled his endorsement of southern priorities and his willingness to use the national government to further regional goals. Wielding the rhetorical tools bequeathed to him by Anti-Federalists and sitting in the seat of national government power, Johnson established the grounds of a long-term agenda for American racial politics.

AN OBSTRUCTIONIST POLITICS TO PRESERVE THE SOUTH ON ITS OWN TERMS

Though many in the North had been initially willing to give Johnson's restoration plan a chance, by the time Congress had reconvened in the fall of 1865, the rejuvenation of the South under the region's former political and military leaders was sufficiently evident for opposition to crystallize. When southern representatives, elected under Johnson's scheme, presented themselves to Congress, their readmission was denied. Under the guidance of leading Radicals, Congress in December of 1865 organized the Joint Committee on Reconstruction to survey conditions in the South and to develop a congressional reconstruction plan as an alternative to the president's. The poles of the conflict were already clear: Johnson's early policy interventions showed decisively that he was going to use the presidency to aid the South, so Congress would deploy its resources to ensure that the victory of the Union in wartime was not squandered.

The result of these efforts was the series of legislation associated with Congressional Reconstruction, including the Freedman's Bureau Bill, the Civil Rights Bill, the Fourteenth and Fifteenth Amendments, and the several Military Reconstruction Acts. The gist of this legislation was to provide legal and material assistance to former slaves transitioning to freedom, to extend citizenship rights to blacks and suffrage to black males, and to eliminate race-based discrimination. The Military Reconstruction Acts, which were administered by district commanders and troops occupying the South, enfranchised black males (prior to ratification of the Fourteenth and Fifteenth Amendments) and disfranchised many former Confederates. They further stipulated that states, to be readmitted to the Union, had to adopt new state constitutions granting universal male suffrage and had to ratify the Fourteenth Amendment. The three states of Texas, Virginia, and Mississippi, all of which lagged in this process, had to additionally ratify the Fifteenth Amendment before being readmitted. Taken together, these congressional acts and amendments signal the defeat of Johnson's agenda and the decline of his presidency for which he is most commonly remembered.[23]

When Johnson's effort to preemptively restore the South to its antebellum status was threatened by congressional action, he turned aggressively to a politics of institutional obstruction in an effort to block enactment of congressional will. As Congress first began to pass Reconstruction legislation, many lawmakers were still interested in working with the president. During this time and even earlier, when Johnson was promoting his restoration agenda, moderate lawmakers repeatedly made overtures to him with strategies designed to build a consensus around modified versions of the president's own policies. Johnson rebuffed every one of these efforts. His immediate and forceful vetoes of their legislation soured the prospect of compromise and drove moderates toward the Reconstruction agenda of the Radicals. For example, Johnson's first veto at this time was of an extension and expansion of the Freedman's Bureau. Lawmakers accepted this veto but subsequently formed a veto-proof majority and consistently overrode later vetoes, including another piece of legislation that accomplished almost all of the same goals as laid out in the original, vetoed Freedman's Bureau bill.[24] Driving moderates toward Radicals secured the passage of Congressional Reconstruction and made Johnson irrelevant to the process of policy production. Yet by responding with an obstructionist politics—including vetoes, reactionary speeches, and disruptive execution of the laws passed by Congress—Johnson continued to advance his aims. He signaled his enduring support for the southern cause, an act not insignificant for a region that had just been militarily defeated. He bought more time for the South to regroup and forced northern lawmakers into an increasingly uncomfortable defense of their actions to a war-weary northern constituency. Last, Johnson's obstructionist politics functioned as a model of opposition strategy for the South. Whether these actions were political miscalculations, as many scholars claim (but a view with which we disagree), or components of a conscious strategy, Johnson's obstinacy, provocation, and subterfuge functioned to provide support and legitimacy to a desperate and defeated region. As we argue below, Johnson's actions were not simply futile efforts of an impotent president but rather sustaining signals from a movement's leader.

Johnson's leadership of the South in opposition to Congressional Reconstruction relied heavily on the weapon of administrative obstruction—a strategy that was hampered by the threat of impeachment but a type of defensive leadership nonetheless. While his earliest executive actions, including those described above, were designed to rejuvenate the politics and economy of the white South, his actions as Congressional Reconstruction progressed focused on subverting the political project of the North. For example, when northern Republicans, invigorated by successes in the 1866 elections, demanded that southern states ratify the Fourteenth Amendment, Johnson encouraged southern leaders to adopt a position of "masterly inactivity." If they refused to cooperate with Reconstruction, he argued, the Republican Party would not press the issue further, and if they did, the unconstitutionality of their actions would be grounds for the president and the courts to intervene. Southern states proceeded to reject the amendment.[25]

Similarly, in the winter of 1866–67, Congress, dissatisfied with conditions in the South and continued obstruction in the region, imposed military Reconstruction, vesting responsibility for its implementation in the hands of district commanders. Johnson was authorized to select the commanders, and he made appointments that were acceptable to Congress. Yet soon after the lawmakers adjourned, he began to replace the more radical commanders with more conservative ones. In addition, the president made an amnesty proclamation in September 1867 that restored the vote to many former Confederate supporters disfranchised by the congressional act.[26]

More than just signaling support of the southern cause, Johnson's vetoes and his manner of executing the laws exercised northern lawmakers and forced them to rely on ever-greater legislative instruction and military implementation and oversight. This required continued justification to a North that believed the war had been won in 1865 and were generally not keen on black suffrage. Republican setbacks in the 1867 elections and the repeated failure of black suffrage referendum votes in northern states was evidence of a growing intolerance in the North for lawmakers' continued efforts on behalf of blacks. Assessing the 1867 election outcomes, the *Nation* declared, "It would be vain to deny that the fidelity of the Republican party to the cause of equal rights . . . has been one of the chief causes of its heavy losses."[27] And this demonstrated to some, Johnson included, that northern political will, ultimately dependent on popular support, was capable of being worn down.[28] In this way, the president's actions, while often unsuccessful in the short run, nonetheless modeled the potential long-term benefits of obstructionist behavior for the South—a lesson learned and repeated, especially in that region, up to the present-day practices of "obstructionist" conservatives in the Republican Party.

Lending credence to this argument is Richard Valelly's insightful analysis of the failure of Congressional Reconstruction. Valelly argues that Congressional Reconstruction failed, in part, because the speed with which northern Republicans expanded their coalition to include southern African Americans made for unstable party building and ultimately led to incomplete institutionalization. According to Valelly, this attempt at "crash party building" was a direct response to the threat from President Johnson's actions, both prior to and after enfranchising blacks. We contend that had Johnson not precipitated this political frenzy, it is feasible that an alternative, enduring coalition building and reconstruction might have taken place. As Richard Bensel points out, Republican difficulties in maintaining their coalition stemmed in part from the fact that none of the party's dominant economic interests was especially vested in Radical Reconstruction. Northern finance capital was most interested in scuttling the Radicals' plan. For a number of immediate and long-term economic reasons, including most notably Reconstruction's interference with the resumption of cotton production and exports, finance capitalists remained loyal to Johnson long after other northern Republicans had deserted him. Bensel's argument about the role played by the finance community in ending Reconstruction is also complementary to our argument. Moderate proposals, which would have satisfied a majority of Republicans and would have more quickly returned the South's cotton fields to production, were abandoned in Congress after Johnson rejected them. By hardening and prolonging radical response, Johnson's actions served to wedge apart the Republican coalition (separating out the Johnson sympathizing finance capitalists from others); and in fueling a key division in the North, his actions helped to close the window of opportunity that Radicals had to enact their agenda.[29]

With the increase in the stringency of the conditions attached to readmittance, the South, too, began to engage in obstructionist behavior. Buoyed by northern Democratic electoral victories, white southern conservatives began in late 1867 to organize and discipline their efforts to defeat ratification of the new state constitutions and thus repudiate Congressional Reconstruction. In Alabama, for example, conservatives encouraged a boycott of the election to ratify the new state constitution in the hopes that the necessary majority of registered voters would not be convened and the vote on the constitution would be nullified.[30] While their efforts failed, they nevertheless are part of the lineage of post–Civil War southern political strategy that extends from "masterly inactivity" in the 1860s to "massive resistance" in the twentieth century.

As African Americans began mobilizing throughout the South, white Southerners' informal yet increasingly systematic methods of opposition to Reconstruction—violence, intimidation, and fraud—increased. Because the exercise of political control by the military had ended with the resumption of the states' civil operations, the army in the South was again under Johnson's full control. With violence escalating, he deferred to local commanders on when and how to respond to state requests for troops to maintain order. Southern Republicans charged that the commanders tended to share Johnson's conservative views and did not provide the degree of support necessary; some Republicans even demanded that Congress reconvene earlier than planned to pass additional Reconstruction legislation.[31] Again, Johnson's actions led to leniency and, in effect, unofficial endorsement of the emerging system of racial order maintenance in the South.[32]

With Grant's election in 1868, Johnson's preemptive and obstructionist efforts in determining the Reconstruction of the South ended, but the struggle to determine the interior life of the South was not over. What had been fought out at the national institutional level was moved to the state level, as the terms the South had been forced to accept were now subject to interpretation on implementation. White conservatives moved quickly to enact economic policies that would ensure continued control over labor in conditions closely approximating plantation life. Some imposed penalties in ways akin to the earlier Black Codes, while others tilted the benefits of the contractual relationship between landlords and sharecroppers squarely toward the planter elite. This economic control continued to be accompanied by violence and the threat of violence.[33] Over the ensuing decades, as the South's racial caste system was reestablished, the effort by the Reconstruction Congress to reverse Johnson's policy was revealed to be nothing more than an interruption in the enactment of his vision. The beneficiary of the ultimate success of his vision was the white South, and these Southerners fortified his unrecognized legacy by extending and further entrenching many of the rhetorical and strategic actions he had launched during his years as president.

As the hallmarks of the Jim Crow South began to emerge, the South not only gained the tools by which to solidify the region's racial order but the strategies for defending against future northern legal and legislative attacks. Massive resistance, the well-known strategy by which white Southerners notoriously defied black civil rights advancements in the twentieth century, is grounded in an understanding of how to accomplish goals through an obstructionist politics, learned by necessity in the aftermath of the Civil War defeat and modeled by President Johnson. New scholarship on the white South's reaction to the North's prosecution of twentieth-century civil rights legislation emphasizes the sophistication of the region's strategic responses. If massive resistance prompted a ratcheting up of northern enforcement, delays and strategic accommodations from white Southerners enabled the region to persevere and mainstream a politics of sustained racial inequalities in contradiction to national and state laws.[34]

Although reasonably well known, several examples of southern obstructionist politics in the arena of civil rights policies are illustrative of the extended, "winning" legacy of Johnson's loss. Southern senators repeatedly used the filibuster (which they preferred to refer to as "an educational campaign") to defeat antilynching legislation in the early decades of the twentieth century. And they famously filibustered, and attached amendments to, civil rights–related legislation in the 1960s, often with an organizational and tactical acumen that allowed them to wear down their opponents. Southern senators also sought to stall civil rights legislation with parliamentary maneuvers such as extended corrections to the previous day's *Senate Journal*, which made an otherwise routine act of unanimous approval a pro-

longed affair that delayed other legislative business. In one instance, with a bill to repeal the poll tax waiting, southern senators
spent five hours on the task of *Journal* correction, with "particular
attention on minute concerns such as the proper placement of
punctuation marks." And in another instance, they refused to approve the *Journal* for twenty-one days to give themselves time
to prepare a successful opposition to legislation to which they
objected.[35]

Another preemptive tactic that white southern political and
economic elites adopted was to appear to accommodate northern
demands so they could maintain as much of the racial order status quo as possible. They pursued this strategy when it was clear
that outright resistance was futile. For example, mid-twentieth-
century elites in Mississippi urged against extremist violence
by white groups so as not to "draw unwanted outside attention,
possibly leading to declarations of martial law."[36] Instead, white
moderates sought what they called "preemptive compromise"
which they used to achieve "some stake in controlling where,
when, and how desegregation would occur."[37] Urging superficial
compliance with national directives, toning down racist rhetoric,
and criticizing hardline segregationists, many moderates pursued
a Janus-faced strategy of "practical segregation" in which they
appeared to embrace integration while allowing segregated practices to reemerge once out of the national spotlight.[38]

These practices are reminiscent of those that Andrew Johnson
pursued nearly a century earlier. It is very plausible that southern
politicians would have deployed an arsenal of preemptive and
obstructionist practices in their attempt to delay or defeat civil
rights legislation without Johnson's leadership. It is also true,
though, that Johnson's obstructionist leadership helped create
the racial order that these senators fought to preserve, and he
exemplified—to a degree few others achieved—the success to
be had with this type of politics. From this vantage point, he
was instrumental in shaping a tradition of southern politics of
obstruction and preemption.

REBUILDING POLITICAL INSTITUTIONS
AND FORTIFYING ALLIES

Providing the South with the opportunity to rebuild and fortify its racial-economic order was a key element of Johnson's policy agenda and a key aspect of his legacy. Yet it would have been meaningless if the region had not had the capacity to sustain itself over time in the political arena. One way that Johnson sought to ensure this was, as described earlier, through the facilitation of the southern states' speedy return to representation in national government. At the same time, Johnson took advantage of the political ambiguity of postwar politics to begin building new political coalitions and networks of allies.

Andrew Johnson was a southern Democrat who assumed office as the result of the assassination of a northern Republican president in the waning moments of the Civil War, and his political position was precarious. On the one hand, Johnson had no natural base of support. Southerners initially viewed him suspiciously because of his wartime loyalty to the Union, and northern Republicans, especially Radicals, were wary of his regional and party roots.[39] On the other hand, with precariousness comes potential. Johnson's political ambitions were focused on the presidency in 1868. Unfettered by party constraints, he was free to build his own coalition to help him in his quest. Given the unique politics of the time, this was an attractive option. Republicans were, for the moment, dominant, but theirs was a new party, tested only on the issue that birthed it: opposition to slavery and secession. A speedy resolution to war issues might sap the wind from the party's sails. Quick restoration of the South would also return that region's Democratic constituency to participation in national government elections. And there were enough Democratic and conservative Republican constituencies in the North that the possibility existed of constructing a new, national, moderate coalition that would return Johnson to the presidency in 1868.

Johnson turned to Secretary of State Seward to help him cultivate this new base of support. Seward was anxious to steer the

Republican Party away from the influence of the Radicals and in a more conservative direction, and this would be a central and legitimating part of the coalition in the North. To this end, the president curried favor with other conservative Republicans as well by distributing among them such patronage-laden posts as the collector of the Port of New York. At the same time, Johnson met and made overtures to top Democrats, in both North and South. In addition to granting clemency to many of the former elite of the South, Johnson sent his political loyalists throughout the region to oversee his restoration efforts and establish contacts. For his efforts, he received assurances from party leaders that the Democratic Party "is today a Johnson party; that the South just as rapidly as his reconstruction plans are carried out, will be a Johnson party."[40]

By 1866, in the face of an increasingly assertive oppositional Congress and a Republican Party that was, itself, in the process of rapid coalition building, Johnson intensified his efforts to build a new coalition by championing the National Union movement, made up of supporters of his restoration policy including Democrats, conservative Republicans, and conservative Southerners. That summer, a National Union convention was held; it was nicknamed the "arm-in-arm" convention after Massachusetts and South Carolina delegates entered the hall in pairs. At the same time, he purged his cabinet of those who did not support this effort (of these, only Secretary of War Stanton, who was sympathetic to Congressional Reconstruction, remained) and in their place appointed conservative Republicans.[41] The movement was defeated in the fall elections that year, but Johnson's political linkages and patronage laid the groundwork on which his allies could continue to build their political network.

This did not stop when Johnson left office. While Republicans in the late 1860s quickly built up a new electoral coalition in part through the enfranchisement of African American men, the party's fortunes were tenuous and provoked reaction. During the 1870s, Republicans were beset by Democratic and southern conservative gains in state governments, usually accomplished through voter intimidation and fraud.[42] Organized intimidation in Alabama in the 1874 election was then successfully copied by other southern states, resulting in the election throughout the region of white Democrats, known as "Redeemers," for the strength of their opposition to the Reconstruction agenda of Radical Republicans. By 1876, Redemption governments were sufficiently ensconced in the South to affect the outcome of the presidential election, disputing returns and forcing the compromise that resulted in the selection of Republican Rutherford B. Hayes as president and the official end of Congressional Reconstruction.[43]

With the withdrawal of military troops, the South achieved the final terms of the war settlement it had sought, and it was free to exercise unencumbered control over its political-economic and racial orders. Within fifteen years, this order, enforced informally since the end of the Civil War, acquired legal form with the full adoption in the 1890s of Jim Crow segregation and restrictive voting laws.[44] The political networks and proto-coalitions spawned by Johnson in the immediate aftermath of the war authorized and legitimated the southern racial order and were, in turn, buoyed by that order. Both had the opportunity to reemerge because of Johnson's early and sustained leadership.

Ideological Disruption and the Provision of New Frames for the South

Johnson's strategy to provide the South, through preemption and obstruction, with the capacity for rebuilding its institutional and political infrastructure was made all the more powerful because he articulated the righteousness of this cause in plausible, sometimes compelling, constitutional arguments. To use language not normally attributed to the post–Civil War white South, Johnson's rhetoric, especially as it developed in opposition to Congressional Reconstruction, were part of his leadership of the politically dispossessed. Owing in no small way to the intellectual heritage carved out by the Anti-Federalist success—which created a tradition of alternative constitutional interpretation—Johnson was able to reasonably position the "dispossessed" South on the side of the Constitution.[45] And because Congress was engaged in a constitutional revolution, arguably in substance and especially in form, Johnson could more easily ally himself and the South with the cause of the original Constitution. As defenders of "the Founders' Constitution," Johnson and the South could claim legitimacy. This then lent authority to his interpretation of the Constitution, much like the way earlier heirs of the Anti-Federalists had claimed authority on the basis of their fidelity to the "framers' Constitution." And, of course, in so doing, Johnson helped to fortify and propagate the mistaken association of Anti-Federal interpretation with the Federalists' understanding of the Constitution.

Johnson vetoed more bills than any of the prior presidents. His first veto was of the Freedman's Bureau bill, passed by Congress in early 1866. The bill extended the life of the wartime agency and authorized its provision of legal and economic assistance (including land and funds for education) to former slaves. In his veto message, Johnson argued against the bureau on the grounds that it would enlarge the scope of the national government and alter the traditional, appropriate balance of federal and state governments. He claimed that the legislation's promotion of the interests of a specific group, former slaves, was unfair because whites had never received such support and that it was unnecessary because blacks now possessed the same economic opportunities as any other group. Last, he argued that the very passage of the bill was illegitimate, because it targeted states that were not yet represented in Congress and so had no say in making the law. These themes—a defense of a states' rights definition of limited government and a heralding of race-neutral individual rights over group rights—dominated Johnson's rhetorical battles with Congress in the ensuing years; they drew on the legitimacy bequeathed by the Anti-Federal appropriation and they became the ideological backbone of southern conservatism to the present day.[46]

Though this was only the first of his many vetoes, Johnson

used the moment to adopt his famously bellicose stance toward Radical lawmakers and Congress's attempts to legislate Reconstruction. A few days after the veto, the president responded to criticisms of his action in an impromptu speech to a crowd of his supporters. In what became known as his "Washington's Birthday Speech," Johnson linked his administration's policy to his staunch support of the Constitution and the Union—the preservation of which was the sole reason for fighting the war.[47] Affirming the necessity of putting an end to southern treason, Johnson then positioned the actions of Radicals, particularly the creation of the guiding hand of the Joint Committee on Reconstruction, as traitorous in its own right:

> One struggle was against an attempt to dissever the Union; but almost before the smoke of the battle-field has passed away—before our brave men have all returned to their homes, and renewed the ties of affection and love to their wives and their children, *we find almost another rebellion inaugurated.* We put down the former rebellion in order to prevent the separation of the States, to prevent them from flying off, and thereby changing the character of our Government and weakening its power. . . . [W]e find now an effort to concentrate all power in the hand of a few at the Federal head, and thereby bring about a consolidation of the Government, *which is equally objectionable with a separation.* We find that powers are assumed and attempted to be exercised of a most extraordinary character. It seems that Governments may be revolutionized—Governments at least may be changed without going through the strife of battle. I believe it is a fact attested in history that sometimes revolutions most disastrous to a people are affected without the shedding of blood. The substance of your Government may be taken away while the form and the shadow remain to you.[48] (italics ours)

Johnson asserted that the actions of the Joint Committee and the legislation passed without representation of the South were as equal a rebellion against the Constitution as the decision to secede. His rhetoric about concentrated power and his leveling of accusations of a dissembling opposition remind one of the alarmed Anti-Federalists during the ratification battle.

His speech did not simply claim for him the righteous action of constitutional preservation against all enemies—though it did do that; it simultaneously pulled the South out of its status as conquered foe, giving to it instead the opportunity for redemption as the new defenders of constitutional propriety. Cloaking narrow southern goals in the language of the Constitution, Johnson's argument made the North the region behaving out of sync with constitutional mandates. Making this point more explicit are Johnson's remarks later on in the speech:

> When those who rebelled comply with the Constitution, when they give sufficient evidence of loyalty, when they show that they can be trusted, when they yield obedience to the law that you and I acknowledge, I say extend to them the right hand of fellowship, and let peace and union be restored. I fought traitors and treason in the South; I opposed the Davises, the Toombes, the Slidells, and a long list of others, which you can readily fill without my repeating the names. Now, when I turn round and at the other end of the line find men—I care not by what name you call them—who still stand opposed to the restoration of the Union of these States, I am free to say to you that I am still in the field.[49]

Note that Johnson moves directly from a defense of the loyal citizens of the South to an accusation of treasonous separatism on the part of northern leaders and an indication of his unfinished battle task (the seamlessness of being "still in the field"). In this and in other messages of the time, including the speeches of his "swing around the circle" tour in the North, Johnson's goal was to put Radicals on the defense and rally popular support behind his course of action. While there were some indications in both the northern and southern press that this was initially successful, by the time of the fall elections, northern voters were rejecting Johnson's interpretation and his program.[50]

Northern rejection, however, is an indication of Johnson's success in signaling to the South his discontent with Congressional Reconstruction and his willingness to work on the region's behalf—a demonstration of sorts of the adage "my enemies' enemy is my friend." His speeches decrying Congress's constitutional transgressions were heralded in the South as of "historical" significance.[51] Johnson's vetoes and speeches provided rhetorical legitimacy to the southern cause, making that region the just defenders of the Constitution, and he used his position of national institutional authority to sustain that side of the ideological dispute.

This was important because Southerners were willing to concede the loss of the secessionist idea as a result of northern military victory, but the accompanying ideas surrounding race and economy had not, for them, been equally vanquished. And although historians today identify Reconstruction as a turning point, a "constitutional moment" in which national government supremacy was firmly established, Southerners at the time were unwilling to forgo the Anti-Federal appropriation of the constitutional mandate, the core aim of which was to preserve state sovereignty. Writing in 1866, southern historian Edward Pollard acknowledged Johnson's role in sustaining southern ideas: "The doctrine of secession was extinguished; and yet there is something left more than the shadow of State Rights, if we may believe President Johnson, who has recently and officially used these terms, and affirmed in them at least some substantial significance."[52]

After Johnson left office, Southerners continued to rely on his ideological fortifications. In the decades following the Civil War, prominent regional spokespersons built on Johnson's initial efforts at reimagining the history and relative significance of southern secession in ways that equated the just natures of the two regions, or at least downplayed their differences. For example, Johnson pointed to "traitors" in both the Civil War South and the Reconstruction North. A decade later, Georgia senator Benjamin Hill, in a widely heralded speech, blamed the war equally on sectionalist elements in both the North and South, obscuring, as Johnson had before him, real differences between the regions' actions and ambitions, before and after the war. Hill decried the loss of the "dear noble boys of the white race, North and South, who fell in the late war, slaying each other for the ne-gro" and reimagined the war as one in which African Americans were the source of the problem, introducing an antagonism be-tween the two (white) regions that need not and should not have arisen.[53] Much as the John Ford cavalry trilogy shows former southern officers, now senior enlisted men, rejoining the cavalry to fight Indians for the greater good of American civilization, Hill's assessment asked his (white) audience to recognize the depth of their similarities and their shared bond of Union and thus forget past acrimonies.[54]

These acts of historical revision sought to rehabilitate the im-age of the South in national memory and obscure the signifi-cance and consequence of postwar regional efforts to, in effect, return to the antebellum status quo. Like Johnson, Hill lauded southern loyalty to the Union. And, like Johnson and others who deployed an Anti-Federal constitutional interpretation cloaked in the legitimacy of the framers' intent, Hill elaborated a states' rights interpretation in which Union was a "system of govern-ment" that ensured liberty by preserving local prerogative. Just as Johnson had cloaked narrow southern goals in the language of the Constitution, Hill's rhetoric, too, further deepened an Anti-Federal narrative of constitutional propriety that was becoming the staple of southern justification of its racial and economic or-der. Although this constitutional interpretation of states' rights had deep roots (as the previous chapter made clear), Johnson was the first president of the post–Civil War era, and as such, his imprimatur resuscitated it from the obscurity to which it might rightly have been destined given the South's military defeat. That Hill and others could continue to build upon it shows how pow-erfully that resuscitation and fortification mattered.

Efforts by southern political representatives to tell the his-tory of the Civil War and Reconstruction in ways that defended the constitutionality of southern actions and benefited white re-gional interests did not end with Hill or with the establishment of Jim Crow, for that matter. Eighty years after Hill's remarks, Richard Russell, a Georgia Democrat and a leader of the "southern bloc," famously spoke against the 1957 civil rights bill, and in that speech, he resurrected "the tragic story of Reconstruction" as northern oppression in order to similarly denounce the 1957 legislative effort. Describing the bill as one to "punish the South," Russell argued that "in all of its implications it is as much of an actual force bill as the measures proposed by Sumner and Stevens in reconstruction days in their avowed drive 'to put black heels on white necks.'" Decrying the power the legislation would invest in the hands of the attorney general, Russell insisted on cross-regional compassion and solidarity, much as Hill and Johnson (and other Southerners) before him had done: "Outside the South," he explained, "there are millions of people who would not approve of another reconstruction at bayonet point of a peaceful and patriotic South. . . . There are many Americans everywhere who would look askance at denying the white people of the South the ordinary rights guaranteed all Americans everywhere, as is proposed in this cunningly contrived bill. There are many Americans who know that constitutional guarantees cannot be denied to the white South without endangering the loss of those guarantees by all the people of this Nation."[55] Russell spoke explicitly and at length in this speech about the purported historic victimization of the white South. But southern politicians resisting desegregation and civil rights legislation throughout the 1950s and 1960s similarly used rhetorical tools bequeathed by the original Anti-Federal appropriation of *The Federalist* to position the South as the defender of constitutionally ensured states' rights against tyrannical federal government action directed by northern elites. In particular, as the cause of civil rights gained steam, southern lawmakers shifted from a reliance on overt racism to defend Jim Crow to, instead, a new "mythology based not on chattel slavery but on the constitutionality of de jure segregation" in which they made claims "in lofty terms as a defense of constitutional principles as wrought by the founders."[56]

This tendency by Johnson and subsequent defenders of the South to reinterpret the historical narrative of the Civil War (the "war of Northern aggression") and its aftermath was more than an abstract exercise in retroactively justifying southern actions. It legitimized ongoing behaviors. When, in the aftermath of Reconstruction, the South moved from relatively informal, local efforts at race control to systematic control fully backed by the legal apparatus of the states, the evolution was justified by looking at national politics and constitutionality through the same prism that Johnson had used. For white Southerners, the abolition of slavery and the prosecution of Congressional Reconstruction did more than simply impose objectionable conditions: it bred chaos and "mob rule." White elites argued for racial solidarity among all whites in reclaiming southern politics on the premise that Reconstruction was, in essence, a northern-fostered slave revolt. While African Americans argued for the ineluctable link between the country's abolition of slavery and the provision of black political rights, white Southerners argued that the North's effort to establish African American political equality was fundamentally illegitimate in a constitutional order premised on white male citizenship.[57] This argument, which justified both white Southerners' resistance to Reconstruction and their demand for the reestablishment of white rule, continued and elaborated the logic of Johnson's argument about northern unconstitutionality. By ascribing to their actions a constitutional vigilance, southern elites maintained the ideological space for their laws and their "order-maintaining" use of violence that was developed earlier by Johnson's rhetoric.[58]

Southerners continued to echo Johnson when they made arguments that elided differences between the regions in order to justify increasing race control and race separation. By the 1890s, for example, southern leaders in Congress were recalling the Black Codes and similar laws as efforts not to monitor blacks but to control labor, comparable to northern vagrancy and apprenticeship laws.[59] Making arguments for race regulation in terms of labor and class may have been a strategy to appeal to northern audiences, but it was also a way of inviting, or insisting on, cross-regional solidarity, much like Johnson's efforts to rally southern and northern loyalists against traitorous Radical lawmakers, Hill's claim of white solidarity, and Russell's arguments about the commitment, shared across regions, to constitutional rights. In other words, creating similarities became a strategy by which Johnson and subsequent southern leaders could legitimize race policies as something else and ward off attention to questionable southern practices. The argument was not a difficult one to make, especially when it came to laws that effectively segregated the races: as southern senators would argue decades later in the mid-twentieth-century school desegregation battles, it was northern states that, in the 1840s, first defended the constitutionality of their region's "separate but equal" schools.[60] Even during Reconstruction, the North had not been insistent on enforcing antisegregation laws. And *Plessy v. Ferguson* in 1896, of course, gave national constitutional legitimacy to "separate but equal."[61]

This tactic of masquerading differences became a trademark of voting restriction legislation. Just as Johnson had argued for race-neutral individual rights over group rights in opposing Reconstruction legislation, arguments were now made in favor of race-neutral educational and property tests for voters. In 1890, Mississippi became the first state to codify an educational qualification in its constitution, and it received the support, not just of Southerners, but of press and politicians from throughout the North as well.[62] That these laws also disenfranchised many poor whites does not diminish the fact that when deployed in the context of the full range of Jim Crow laws, blacks were primary targets for disfranchisement.[63]

When Northerners in Congress first began their task of Reconstruction in the 1860s, they were under the sway of an influential Republican lawyer from Boston, Richard Dana, who argued that the North should use the instrument of national government to hold the South "in the grasp of war" until it had extracted from the vanquished region all that it justly deserved as the fruits of its victory.[64] This justified an expansion of the capacity of the national government and a reliance on the military until the South had submitted to northern demands. This northern plan for Reconstruction was ultimately unsuccessful. Whether out of a sense of moral justice or out of an interest in securing the region politically, the North's demand that the South reconstitute its social, economic, and political order to give blacks a fair and equal place ultimately failed. Indeed, bolstered by Andrew Johnson's leadership—his legitimating rhetoric, his strategic lessons, the capacity-building space he cleared with his preemptive and obstructionist politics, and the lifeline to national government he provided while the region was disfranchised—the South more effectively executed Dana's strategy. With Johnson's early encouragement and fortified by the Anti-Federal appropriation, the South held the North in "the grasp of war," a guerrilla war to be sure but a war nonetheless, until it wearied of the effort of attempting to impose its will. Analyzing the class politics of the time, Eric Foner has written that Reconstruction began with the South trying to adjust to the North's system of free labor and ended with the North accepting the South's understanding of labor-capital conflict.[65] The same could be said of the evolution of the regions with regard to race relations: the attempts to impose a more egalitarian racial politics on the South ended with the North's tacit acceptance of the other region's system of racial order management.

The legacy of Andrew Johnson's loss was secured with the full codification of Jim Crow and northern acceptance of the South's practices. But the power of that legacy is perhaps best evidenced by its profound influence on Woodrow Wilson, a Southerner who was also a twentieth-century progressive. In the previous chapter, we explained how the powerful but unrecognized influence of the Anti-Federal appropriation led Wilson to mischaracterize the framers' ambitions and thus cast his policies as fixes to the Constitution's deficits when, in actuality, his proposals were entirely in keeping with the political logic of the Constitution. With the evidence presented in this chapter, we can see how Johnson's inflection on the Anti-Federal legacy explains the apparent contradiction between Wilson's progressive democracy commitments and his racist policies—a contradiction that has befuddled many observers. In an article titled "The Reassociation of Ideas and Purposes: Racism, Liberalism, and the American Political Tradition," Stephen Skowronek describes the conceptual "interpenetration of antithetical ends" through which Wilson formulated and advocated modern liberal ideals, including notions of democracy and national consensus, to advance racist ends. As Skowronek explains, Wilson repudiated Johnson's leadership style yet hewed closely to the earlier president's regional outlook and animating political objectives. Like a long line of southern politicians going back to Johnson, Wilson saw northern Reconstruction lawmakers as having instituted a dangerous new democratic order, one in which an empowered northern majority had overturned "constitutional limits" on government in order to impose an ill-conceived program of rights.[66] Through a reworking of the ideas of democracy and a defense of local prerogative and accommodationist politics, Wilson further sanitized—and therefore broadened and legitimized—southern reliance on the rhetorical resources of the Anti-Federal appropriation, using the post-ratification Anti-Federal constitutional interpretation as a means to advance specific regional interests.[67] This particular "reassociation" of national liberal ideas with regional purposes would not have been possible without Johnson's initial ideological groundwork in the face of Congressional Reconstruction.

Though Johnson's actions to restore the South as much as possible to an antebellum status quo were often thwarted and though they led to his impeachment, they are not simply indications of his failure as a president. What he did successfully with his preemptive efforts on behalf of the South, his obstructionist politics, and his dogged rhetoric was to lay the groundwork for and guide southern states toward ultimate victory: a return to the Union with the freedom to determine their own socioeconomic order. Southern conservative leaders acknowledged the defeat of slavery, but they refused to accommodate in any but the most superficial of ways the additional demands placed upon them by northern lawmakers. And in the end, they prevailed—for more than one hundred years at least. The collapse of Congressional

Reconstruction in the 1870s removed the last barrier to the institution of the Jim Crow South, complete with the political disfranchisement, economic subjugation, and social segregation of African Americans that white Southerners had been seeking since the end of the war.

New Deal
Barry Goldwater's
Politics of Integrity

It is hard to overstate the hegemony of New Deal liberalism in 1960. Nearly thirty years after the New Deal constitutional moment, the nation's commitment to core regime principles, institutions, and policies, including social security, the Tennessee Valley Authority, minimum wage, welfare, agricultural price supports, aid to education, deficit financing of national programs, and multilateral internationalism, was still powerful enough to induce even President Eisenhower, a Republican, to expand the New Deal agenda rather than oppose it. Eisenhower founded the Department of Health, Education and Welfare, defended social security, and built an interstate highway system. He joined with Democrats in sustaining a bipartisan consensus on Cold War containment policy toward the Soviet Union.[1] All of these policies had their origins in the New Deal Democratic transformation of American politics, which strengthened and deployed new forms of national administrative power in both foreign and domestic policy arenas. As a result of the success of the New Deal revolution, Eisenhower, and other successful Republicans in the middle of the twentieth century, talked and behaved like Democrats. This fact led prominent scholars of the time to lament the "tweedle dee, tweedle dum" nature of American political parties.[2]

No fact better establishes the hegemony of New Deal liberalism than the defeat of Barry Goldwater in the 1964 presidential contest. Unlike most other prominent Republicans of the time, Goldwater pointedly objected to every element of the New Deal agenda: its principles were unconstitutional; its practices and policies were unwise; and its complex of principles, practices, and institutions were dangerous to the health and future of freedom. Goldwater ran against the New Deal regime, but his campaign theme, "A Choice, not an Echo," was as much a rebuke to the Republican leadership at the time as it was a challenge to Democrats. This rebuke and challenge was incomprehensible to mainstream observers of the campaign: "When, in all our history, has anyone with ideas so bizarre, so archaic, so self-confounding, so remote from the basic American consensus, ever got so far?" wondered Richard Hofstadter on the eve of the election.[3] Others who were more sympathetic to Goldwater's views than Hofstadter nonetheless acutely understood how the candidate's blunt rejection of the New Deal consensus would affect the Republican Party's chance at the presidency. Richard Nixon described feeling "almost physically sick" upon hearing Goldwater cite his famous convention line: "I would remind you that extremism in the defense of liberty is no vice. And let me remind you also that moderation in the pursuit of justice is no virtue." And Pat Buchanan proclaimed that Goldwater's statement, "dealt the ace of trumps to a Democratic campaign that already had a fistful of trumps to play."[4]

Goldwater's vision was rejected in a landslide defeat. With the exception of Alfred Landon's 1936 loss to FDR, Goldwater's was the biggest popular loss in American presidential history. Lyndon Baines Johnson (LBJ) won more than 60 percent of the popular vote nationwide and more than 90 percent of the nation's electoral votes. He won all but six states and most by staggering margins. Democrats everywhere had lopsided victories.

The rout led media commentators to announce the death of political conservatism in America: "Barry Goldwater not only lost the presidential election yesterday but the conservative cause as well. . . . He has wrecked his party for a long time to come and is not even likely to control the wreckage," wrote James Reston of the *New York Times*.[5] Many Republicans saw in the defeat a lesson about the viability of conservatism. In a rebuke to Goldwater's brand of conservativism, the head of the New York Republican Party said the defeat was a "shattering price" paid by the party for its "erratic deviation from our soundly moderate 20th-century course."[6] As we described in chapter 1, winning, in the conventional sense, in the two-party system has typically required a drive toward the stable and moderate center; for many Republicans at the time, the 1964 fiasco seemed to underscore this truism.

Yet just sixteen years later Ronald Reagan won the presidency in a landslide of similar proportions and New Deal hegemony was over. As columnist George Will quipped about the conservative era that followed, it was actually Goldwater who had won; "it just took 16 years to count the votes."[7] And, indeed, the overarching public philosophy and many of the policy positions for which Goldwater had so disastrously campaigned, including a more robust defense state and a restoration of states' rights, became the new norm after 1980. The label "conservative" quickly replaced "liberal" as the politically advantageous moniker. "Tax and spend" liberalism had become a dirty phrase. In 1994, conservative Republicans led their party's successful effort to wrest Congress from a decades-long Democratic dominance. Even Democratic president Bill Clinton got on the bandwagon, announcing that the era of "big government" was over. In highly symbolic moves, Clinton in 1996 signed the repeal of Aid to Families with Dependent Children, a cornerstone program of his party's welfare state, and in 1999 he signed the repeal of the Glass-Steagall Act, banking regulation legislation first enacted by his party in 1933—two measures that, to conservatives, represented all that was wrong about New Deal redistributive and regulatory activism. It is our contention that this dramatic turn of events was not just an ironic outcome of Goldwater's defeat; rather, it was a result of that defeat itself. We mean to argue, in other words, that the very decisions that led to Barry Goldwater's massive political defeat facilitated the long-term influence of his political vision several decades later.

We proceed in the sections below by highlighting four mechanisms responsible for Goldwater's loss that subsequently served as the foundation upon which Republicans would construct the modern conservative era. First, Goldwater's campaign introduced the nation to the conservative critique of New Deal liberalism and to a genuinely alternative public philosophy. Second, Goldwater's reluctant leadership energized conservative activists to build an organizational infrastructure outside of the mainstream Republican Party that had the capacity not only to sustain itself beyond his defeat but to become a force with which to be reckoned. Third, Goldwater's display of the principles and rhetoric necessary to unite disparate constituencies into a new South- and West-based coalition provided electoral strategies to subsequent Republican Party leaders. Last, Goldwater's temperament and his refusal to conduct himself like a "typical politician" ensured the coherence of the ideological, organizational, and strategic lessons bequeathed to his successors, thus allowing for the rapid resurrection of his conservative vision.

These four attributes of Goldwater's campaign ensured his loss in 1964, yet they were also the mechanisms by which conservative Republicans were subsequently able to achieve national success. In making the case that these features should be considered together as the mechanisms by which loss was converted to success, our aim is greater than simply presenting Goldwater as a neglected leader of modern conservatism, though this alone would be a challenge to a substantial body of existing scholarship. Unlike early accounts that described, or dismissed, conservative intellectual thought or reactionary "fringe" movements, recent work has focused on documenting the ways that grassroots activism transformed the national political landscape from the ground up.[8] In these accounts, Goldwater is typically treated in one of three ways. He is at times seen as a setback to movement success because of his alleged extremism and embarrassing defeat. Alternatively, he is sometimes depicted as a leader before his time whose presence was ultimately incidental to the later success of the movement. A third view, related to the second, accords him a greater leadership role for how his campaign inspirited the movement that went on to subsequently achieve success. Our view most closely accords with this last perspective.[9] But by showing how Goldwater's agency—namely, his decision to campaign with an acute political integrity, evident in all four mechanisms described above—led to both his 1964 loss and his subsequent success, we believe we go well beyond the most generous of the existing arguments, which suggest that his leadership amounted to merely rousing the faithful.

We aim to show that Goldwater's leadership was central to the success of the antimoment of New Deal liberalism. Yet in describing how Goldwater's conduct and actions helped to ensure his loss and eventual success, we also contend with the limits of his success. The limits here are more evident than in our earlier two cases. Modern conservatism did prevail just sixteen years after his initial defeat, and yet there are ideological and policy currents of conservatism today that Goldwater repudiated before he died—not because he had changed, but because, building on his foundation, Republican leaders had taken conservatism in a direction that was afoul of his principles. We conclude with an assessment of the political significance of Goldwater's integrity and the complex legacy of his loss.

"A Choice, Not an Echo": Forging an Alternative Public Philosophy

As is well known, the most prominent Republican leaders in the 1950s and early 1960s, including President Eisenhower, Vice President (and 1960 presidential candidate) Richard Nixon, and Senator Nelson Rockefeller, preached a moderate Republicanism. They accepted, supported, and promoted policies in line with the basic tenets of the New Deal regime's public philosophy. In doing so, they created a bipartisan consensus for national government activism in pursuit of economic growth and a qualified social justice as well as for a vigilant but flexible containment policy to deal with Soviet power. Appalled by this bipartisan harmony, conservative critics despaired that the differences between the two parties were of degree, not of kind. Conservative journalist and *Straight Talk* columnist Tom Anderson lamented that the two major parties were more appropriately named "Socialist Party A and Socialist Party B."[10]

Barry Goldwater's stalwart conservatism represented a marked departure from the liberal consensus. Elected to the Senate in 1952, Goldwater chastised the Republican program under Eisenhower as a "dime store New Deal." He took unpopular stances on bipartisan votes that were of high salience to the public, including voting against the censure of Senator Joseph McCarthy in 1954, against the Kennedy-Ervin Labor Reform Bill in 1959, and against the Civil Rights Act of 1964. Contemplating a presidential run in 1963, he discussed launching a cross-country presidential debate tour with President Kennedy, with whom he disagreed but liked personally, in order to hash out publicly their clear policy and ideological disagreements.[11] All of these actions were consistent with Goldwater's belief that the Republican challenge to Democrats should not center on who could provide a more efficient New Deal but on the infirmities of the beliefs of the New Deal itself. He understood that principled debate before the American public was necessary to give meaning to democratic governance. Ironically, Goldwater shared with progressive political scientists an appreciation for what a democratically responsible party system should look like—one that provided programmatic choice, and with it government accountability.[12]

Goldwater's enthusiasm for the 1964 presidential race disappeared after Kennedy's assassination, but he was persuaded by conservative activists to pursue the Republican nomination nonetheless. In both the Republican primary and the general campaign, Goldwater stood fast on the conservative principles to which he was committed and which were outlined in *Conscience of a Conservative*. Ghostwritten by L. Brent Bozell Jr. and self-published by a conservative outlet created for this purpose (Clarence Manion's Victor Publishing), Goldwater's 1960 book outlined a public philosophy alternative to the New Deal liberal program. In it, Goldwater went beyond arguing policy specifics to crafting a political philosophy premised on an alternative understanding of the nature of man and the relationship between individual and society. Unlike most books written to introduce a presidential aspirant, where the ideas serve to legitimize the stature of the aspirant, *Conscience* was written to elevate the status of the political ideas themselves.[13] In *Conscience*, Goldwater *is* the ideas Goldwater represents; they are not attributes of a biographical story. Written as the campaign manifesto, the book was designed to express what Goldwater stood for, not where he came from. And to be clear, Goldwater was not simply some vessel upon which enterprising operatives could foist their desired political philosophy or narrative. Although the book was ghostwritten by Bozell, the text came from the candidate's earlier speeches, and Goldwater edited each chapter.[14]

In outlining conservative principles and policy objectives, Goldwater sought to fashion an ideology free of apologies. He chastised Republicans like Nixon, who insisted on *qualifying* his conservatism, and those like Rockefeller, who called himself a *progressive* Republican. It is Goldwater's unadulterated proclamation of conservatism at a time when New Deal ideology still reigned supreme that sets it apart as a true public philosophy alternative. In urging the Republican Party to abandon its apologetic stance and endorse a clear alternative, Goldwater aimed to fundamentally redefine the political order, just as FDR had done thirty years earlier—and as Ronald Reagan would do sixteen years later. What is perhaps most astonishing is that this comprehensive and coherent ideology was laid out *before* Goldwater made his run for the presidency. By comparison, the New Deal philosophy was only articulated after the elections of 1932 and 1936, in the midst of FDR's crisis governance, one that was self-described not as a political philosophy but as the result of "bold persistent experimentation."[15] To find a similar instance in American history in which a public philosophy preceded a presidential campaign and reordered American politics, one would have to return to Thomas Jefferson's election in 1800, when, as we suggest in chapter 2, he reappropriated Anti-Federal prescriptions (and appropriated *Federalist* rhetoric) for the new nation.

Conscience set forth the idea that preserving and nurturing human individuality is both in accord with Nature and of first priority politically. Goldwater criticized liberals (and socialists) for focusing too exclusively on the material needs of humans and for naïvely relying on the state to overcome human differences. He argued instead for a restoration of Nature as a standard that would return to political priority both the material and also the spiritual dimensions of human experience. Conservatism had been wrongly defended as an economic theory, he argued, and he cast it instead as attending to the totality of what it means to be human: "The root difference between the Conservatives and the Liberals of today is that Conservatives take account of the *whole* man, while the Liberals tend to look only at the material side of man's nature." It is from this capacious view that he built a strong yet socially responsible case for individual liberty.

Conscience of a Conservative detailed the key principles and policy implications of this philosophy. A true though unknowing Anti-Federal heir, Goldwater appealed for a restoration of the understanding of the Constitution as a charter for limited government. In sharp contrast to FDR's call for the constitutional necessity of an "economic bill of rights" that would mandate state expansion, Goldwater hearkened back to an interpretation of the Constitution, dominant before the New Deal, as a limit on government. Stressing the significance of the Tenth Amendment, Goldwater, like Andrew Johnson and other Anti-Federalist heirs before him, argued for the constitutional propriety of states' rights. Urging attention to the importance of individual initiative and responsibility, Goldwater called for reduced taxation to match reduced functions of government. He demanded an end to almost all forms of federal subsidies, ranging from agriculture to welfare, as they subjugated the individual to the state.[16] He opposed monopoly power of any kind, including that of labor unions which he claimed exploited workers as much as if not more than employers. Generally, he envisioned a reduction of government so as to foster self-reliance among individuals, families, and local communities.

Goldwater's views on civil rights were more nuanced than often acknowledged, yet they drew logically from his fundamental commitment to limited national government. He argued that federal power, as constitutionally specified, should be exercised to protect the right to vote and the right to hold property, to ensure equal treatment before the law, and to protect contracts. But he argued against federal intervention into areas such as education and privately owned businesses, thus leading him (infamously) to oppose federal desegregation efforts.[17]

In contrast, Goldwater viewed defense as the primary responsibility of national government, and therefore urged a more robust response in the fight against communism than the Republican Party had previously championed. He criticized the reigning objective of "peace" via containment, which, he argued, failed to see the enemy as an enemy fully intent on its stated ambitions of world domination. Rather than coexistence, Goldwater urged mobilization to defeat Soviet Communism. Among other policies, this committed him to arguing for the cessation of aid to communist countries, a stern approach to Castro's Cuba, the bolstering and enlargement of military alliances, a refusal to recognize the Kruschev regime, and an increase in military preparedness, including the tactical use of nuclear weaponry.

Goldwater's unabashed commitment to these conservative principles mobilized his supporters but doomed his presidential campaign. In April of 1964, Phyllis Schlafly released *A Choice Not an Echo* urging conservative activists and Republican delegates to reject the party establishment in favor of a conservative like Goldwater. Spurred on by successful grassroots organization and despite ominous warnings from mainstream politicians and media, party delegates nominated Goldwater to run against Kennedy's successor, President Lyndon Johnson. Yet as historian Donald Critchlow and others describe, from the beginning of the general election campaign, even Goldwater staffers knew the race was hopeless.[18] Aside from the impact on the race of Kennedy's assassination, the ideology of the New Deal was sufficiently hegemonic in 1964 that Goldwater's ideas were too incomprehensible and threatening to ordinary voters to sway their views. The taint of extremism put on Goldwater and his ideas by LBJ's campaign ads did not help, but the ideas themselves were simply too foreign to most voters. Pilloried by other Republicans in the primary race, demonized by Democrats in the general campaign, Goldwater never stood a chance.

Goldwater offered a clear, unequivocal ideological alternative and this ensured his massive electoral loss, yet that very outcome paved the way for the resurrection of conservatism sixteen years later under Ronald Reagan. The rejection of his ideas helped the subsequent rise of conservatism in two ways: his defeat facilitated the temporary success of Johnson's ambitious extension of the New Deal agenda, and it provided a new civic lens the public could use to evaluate and eventually repudiate LBJ's Great Society.

The rout of Goldwater opened a political window through which President Johnson could pursue his ambitious agenda. Leading up to his landslide victory, Johnson had approval ratings above the 70th percentile, and the election that gave him a new term as president also sent an influx of liberal Democrats to Congress. These developments allowed him to act as if he had a clear electoral mandate for his desired policy changes. Having secured passage of the Civil Rights Act prior to the election, Johnson proceeded with the vast array of Great Society and War on Poverty programming. As conservative commentator David Frum has lamented, "Goldwater's overwhelming defeat invited a tsunami of liberal activism."[19] Had Nelson Rockefeller won the Republican nomination in 1964, it is unlikely that LBJ would have won the presidency by such a substantial margin nor garnered as much new support in Congress. It is therefore at least possible, if not likely, that Johnson would have been thwarted in his efforts to realize the full scope and ambition of his domestic agenda. It is also possible that had Johnson been forced into accepting a more modest agenda it would have been more successful, politically, over the long run.

In addition to what Goldwater's defeat enabled Johnson to do, Goldwater's ideological alternative to the New Deal educated the polity on how to read the eventual shortcomings and failures of Great Society programming. Perhaps unwittingly, the American public learned how to view the world differently in 1964. Had Nelson Rockefeller, William Scranton, or Henry Cabot Lodge Jr. been the Republican nominee (all possible alternatives), the American public would not have been introduced to conservative ideology. Reflecting on the election many years later, Harry Jaffa, the conservative scholar who helped write Goldwater's nomination acceptance speech—the same speech that cemented his "extremist" label—conceded that he never expected Goldwater to win but that he "thought of the Goldwater campaign as an attempt to educate the American people and the conservative movement itself."[20] Without that education, the public would not have been prompted to view the elaboration of the New Deal as its decay. In the context of liberal overreach in the latter half of the 1960s—with unmet expectations at home and abroad producing social upheaval and political violence—the ideas so recently and soundly dismissed as incomprehensible became the key to facilitating a negative evaluation of President Johnson and the direction in which the country appeared to be headed. Stephen Skowronek has written insightfully about how presidents are, in part, products of their times. "Reconstructive" presidents, often considered "great" presidents because of their capacity to change the partisan political order, are so in part because they have an electorate that is ready for new ideas, while "disjunctive" presidents, often seen as "failures," are so in part because the electorate has grown disillusioned with the partisan regime to which that president is affiliated. In our view, Goldwater's 1964 educational presidential campaign prepared the electorate for its rejection of the New Deal order under Carter and its eventual embrace of Reagan Republicanism.[21]

Conservative ideology provided the framework for a critique of New Deal liberalism, but for it to appeal to voters as a public philosophy in its own right, complete with new institutional, policy, and programmatic implications, required a new generation of Republican leadership. As the next two sections make clear, that leadership, from both the ground up and the top down, had been groomed by the experiences of the Goldwater campaign. Conservatives made some headway with Richard Nixon's opportunistic embrace of their rhetoric and goals in 1968. But Ronald Reagan's speech on behalf of Goldwater during the 1964 campaign and his election to the California governorship in 1966 helped make him conservatives' favored successor to Goldwater. It was his election to the presidency in 1980 that would ultimately reorder American politics.

Building the Conservative Organization and Taking Over the Party

"We are conservatives. This great Republican Party is our historic house."

These were Goldwater's words to the Republican convention in 1960, when he advised conservatives to "grow up" and begin the work of taking back the Republican Party from the moderate establishment, as he thought they could. In 1960, that looked like an impossible task to most. But four years later, Goldwater and fellow conservatives successfully captured the Republican nomination. In this sense, as is often acknowledged, 1964 represents the watershed year in which the locus of control of the Republican Party shifted from the eastern establishment to the party's conservative faction.[22] Goldwater, himself, however, was reluctant to head the Republican ticket, and because of this, conservative activists were forced to develop organizational capacities to recruit him and to secure his nomination. Their success ensured the party's defeat in the general campaign, but it also provided a lasting organizational infrastructure and campaign techniques that would benefit future Republicans (and eventually, in 2008, even a Democrat). It is our contention that had Goldwater not been the reluctant candidate that he was, this chain of events may not have occurred as it did.

Much has been made of the activities of a handful of conservative ideologues, thinkers, and strategists, including Clifton White, William Rusher, John Ashbrook, William Buckley, Clarence Manion, William Baroody, and L. Brent Bozell, who orchestrated the Goldwater nomination over establishment candidate Nelson Rockefeller.[23] As early as 1961, many of these young conservatives began to develop the network and infrastructure that would deliver delegates to Goldwater in 1964. Under William Baroody's leadership, the American Enterprise Institute (AEI) emerged as one of the nation's influential policy think tanks and began producing much of the intellectual argument behind Goldwater's campaign. Through association with AEI and with *National Review*, through key organizations such as the Young Republicans and the Young Americans for Freedom, and through the launch of the Draft Goldwater Committee, movement activists began to cultivate conservatives in precincts around the country, but especially in the South and West.[24] As Lee Edwards describes it, "Goldwater was charismatic, unapologetically conservative, and unambiguously guided by principle. For him, principle, not power, was the core of politics. Such a personality proved successful in bringing the South and the West, and the young and the energetic, into the GOP and the conservative movement for the first time."[25]

The political operation of these movement activists was unprecedented. They mapped district-level demographic and voting trends, developed fund-raising mailing lists, and targeted small donors in their effort to secure the nomination for Goldwater. By doing so, they introduced techniques that would become the hallmark of modern political campaigns.[26] They self-published and expertly marketed books to promote conservative ideals to a broad audience, including Schlafly's *A Choice Not an Echo*, John Stormer's *None Dare Call It Treason*, and J. Evetts Haley's *A Texan Looks at Lyndon: A Study of Illegitimate Power*. None was more successful, though, than *Conscience of a Conservative*, originally published in 1960 by Victor Publishing, "the dummy imprint [Clarence Manion] had set up and licensed as a Kentucky based not-for-profit" for the sole purpose of marketing Goldwater's ideas.[27] Decrying the era's political leadership, outlining conservatism, and promoting Goldwater's candidacy, these books were widely circulated.[28] By November 1964, *Conscience of a Conservative* had sold more than 3.5 million copies and was a *New York Times* bestseller.[29] Once at the Republican convention in San Francisco, Goldwater's team deployed new communication technologies and organizational infrastructure to direct delegates, pass information on the convention floor, and mobilize supporters to action.[30]

Movement activists secured the nomination for Goldwater by organizing outside of and against the party establishment. More than simply competing for delegates against mainstream candidates, these activists also, and first, had to mobilize to secure Goldwater's commitment. Conservatives had identified Goldwater as the standard-bearer of conservatism in 1960, yet he was a reluctant candidate at best. He was a committed conservative, and he had no desire to make the sort of compromises to his principles in the way that politicians typically must to secure votes from a general public. In December of 1963, marveling at his failure to commit to running with just six months to go to the Republican convention, journalists Rowland Evans and Robert Novak wrote, "If Goldwater were an ordinary politician, there is no question that he would go after the nomination. He remains the man with the most delegates. . . . Never before has a frontrunner removed himself from the running. But Goldwater is not the run-of-the-mill presidential candidate. He has neither love for political campaigning nor burning ambition to become president."[31]

At the same time, he did not rebuff conservative overtures. When Manion told Goldwater that conservatives wanted to organize a campaign for him, the senator "assured us that he would not at any time repudiate the move."[32] Goldwater's qualified encouragement convinced conservatives that their efforts might be rewarded, but his ambivalence forced them to rally the faithful to convince him to run—in short, they had to draft Goldwater. Doing so meant demonstrating to him the depth and breadth of unalloyed conservative support, along the way organizing the machinery needed to win the nomination. As he contemplated his run in 1963, Goldwater, who, according to Evans and Novak, felt a "special sense of responsibility as leader-symbol of the grassroots conservative movement," wanted first and foremost for his actions to help, and not hurt, the movement. And when word got out that Goldwater might ultimately not run, his office was "barraged . . . with an unprecedented volume of telegrams and letters urging him to run."[33] Despite his hesitations, especially after Kennedy's assassination, Goldwater felt he owed it to his supporters to run and in January of 1964 announced his candidacy as a conservative Republican. As he later reflected, "Instinctively, intuitively, I knew that the commitment—the bond I had made to so many conservatives and they to me—was virtually unbreakable at this point. It was all over. I said 'All right, damn it, I'll do it.'"[34]

Precisely because they mobilized the right successfully enough to convince Goldwater to lead and to secure for him the Republican nomination, the conservative machinery doomed his candidacy to failure in the general election. Tailored to capture the nomination, conservative organizational innovations were ill-suited to the general election given the preferences and opinions of the electorate overall. A more moderate general electorate was turned off by the zeal Goldwaterites had demonstrated in the primaries and at the Republican convention, what one

Goldwater biographer has termed "the Woodstock of American conservatism."[35] Biographer Rick Perlstein recounts a number of the more exuberant conservative movement displays, especially at the convention. For example, he writes that while the Republican National Committee's (RNC) rules and platform were being read aloud, Goldwaterites began a ritual in which "one side of . . . [the] hall would raise the earsplitting cry 'VIVA!' The other side, challenged to scream louder, pronounced: 'OLE!'" Reporting for *Esquire*, Norman Mailer described hearing "a mystical communion in the sound even as Sieg Heil used to offer its mystical communion." And when Rockefeller attempted to warn the convention about the dangers of an extremist takeover of the party, he was booed and drowned out by chants of "We Want Barry!"[36] Although Goldwater distanced himself from some conservative organizations—for example, shifting campaign management to loyalists from Arizona as the campaign heated up—it was too late.[37] The public's initial skepticism of conservative ideology was reinforced by the efforts of, first, the Rockefeller campaign and, then, the Democratic Party to paint Goldwater as an extremist—a warmonger and racist.

Had Goldwater conformed to the standard political science description of a politician—a rational and ambitious office seeker—conservatives may not have had to develop the organizational capacity nor mobilize as they did to convince him of the existence of their support. Had he been a rationally behaving office seeker, Goldwater would have also adopted moderate positions and thus would not have spurred conservative supporters to sustained action. And while their efforts cost Goldwater the election, they created an organizational infrastructure and the grassroots ideological support for that structure that could last beyond their candidate. The energy, organization, and technological campaign innovations first developed to recruit Goldwater's leadership became crucial to Republican candidates' successes in future elections up through the present.[38]

The Strategy for an "Emerging Republican Majority"

In 1960, Richard Nixon campaigned as a moderate Republican in all fifty states.[39] By 1968, he had moved significantly to the right, campaigning with rhetoric that was notably more conservative and targeted to states in the South and West. While much had changed in the country in the eight-year interim, Nixon had also changed—the result of the Goldwater campaign in 1964. Goldwater's success with conservatives had doomed his candidacy in 1964. Yet what this taught Nixon was the need both to court conservatives and to forge linkages between them and a broader coalition.[40] The 1964 election not only provided tactical lessons that helped Nixon win the presidency in 1968 but it also provided the rhetorical tools and long-range strategic insights with which first Nixon and then Reagan would build the broader Republican coalition over the next several decades.

Perhaps the most important strategic lesson to emerge from 1964 was awareness of the prospects for cultivating a new Republican base in the South and West. Much has already been made of Richard Nixon's "southern strategy" and the Republican Party's electoral conversion of the South from a Democratic stronghold to a Republican one. While Johnson's actions on civil rights irreparably damaged the Democratic Party coalition, Nixon is the president credited with successfully capitalizing on this and beginning the Republican Party's courtship of the South in earnest.[41] Under the tutelage of campaign consultant Kevin Phillips, author of *The Emerging Republican Majority*, Nixon in 1968 sought to build a new Republican coalition by appealing to states in the South and West. "Who needs Manhattan when we can get the electoral votes of eleven southern states?" Phillips said in 1968. "Put those together with the Farm Belt and the Rocky Mountains, and we don't need the big cities."[42] Phillips amassed reams of demographic and voting data to back up his strategic suggestions, but his advice to Richard Nixon was compelling, in large part, because of the evidence supplied by Barry Goldwater and the 1964 presidential race.

As an Arizonan, Goldwater embodied a sense of practical, rugged individualism that was characteristically western. Lee Edwards, the director of information for the Goldwater campaign, described Goldwater as an "Arizona businessman with a strong Western independent streak favoring self-reliance, old fashioned get-off-my-back, out-of-my-pocket kind of spirit that you had in the frontier West."[43] One might call this his "gut conservatism," and it lent authenticity to his ideological and philosophical views.[44] Departing from Nixon's 1960 effort to appeal to moderates everywhere, Goldwater in 1964 courted the West and the South with a campaign that was a good match for the emerging Sunbelt. States on the cutting economic edge, going through a rapid economic boom and demographic change, had a fresh and forward-looking self-identification, and Goldwater personified the rugged individualism and opportunity that was the imprint of the West on the mythic American national identity.[45] Goldwater's frontier mentality, for example, provided authenticity to his aggressive anticommunism.[46] This stance appealed to Sunbelt defense industries and to members of the John Birch Society, whose growth was most rapid in the Sunbelt and with whom he maintained a careful, distanced relationship.[47] Thus, more than simply a statement of abstract principles, his ideology resonated in western and southern states because it was so regionally inflected.

Goldwater's regional sensibilities and business experience drove his antipathy toward the East and his criticism of both the Democratic Party and the moderate, northeastern leadership of his own party.[48] This, too, resonated in the South and West because of their shared history of antagonism toward a perceived domination by the northeastern political and financial elite. As Stewart Alsop wrote for the *Saturday Evening Post* in 1963, "Another key to the Goldwater phenomenon is what sociologists have called the 'revolt of the South and West.' That revolt is now complete. The era when the South and West were semi-colonial dependencies of New York-dominated capital is over, but in these areas 'the East' is still regarded with a mixture of suspicion, dislike and envy. Goldwater perfectly expresses this attitude—to an extent hardly recognized in the East, he is the anti-Eastern candidate. He once remarked—perhaps only half jokingly—that the East Coast ought to be 'sliced off and set adrift.'"[49] In the 1964 campaign, Goldwater argued that he was "just 'old-fashioned' enough to believe that people—not bureaucrats, not self-styled experts, not self-anointed wise-men—but plain people, and their elected representatives, know best what their needs are and how best they may be served."[50] This populist tone fueled resentment of the New Deal's centralized authority, top-down planning, and bureaucracy that would emerge prominently in later elections, especially in the South and West. Despite its characteristically western rhetorical flair, this comment, and others like it, resonated as well with the ideological defense of states' rights that white Southerners had long used in their effort to preserve their region's racial order. Goldwater's campaign had fresh appeal to conservative white Democrats in the region because of the growing disgruntlement with the embrace of black civil rights by the northern wing of their party (Strom Thurmond, for example, converted from Democrat to Republican in 1964).

Goldwater's anti-"big government" rhetoric energized conservatives and helps to explain not only his win in Arizona and the five states of the Deep South (South Carolina, Georgia, Mississippi, Alabama, and Louisiana) but also why Johnson's margin of victory was generally much smaller in states in the South and West than in the North. Tellingly, whereas Republican presidential candidates since Lincoln had received up to a third of the black vote, Goldwater received just 4 percent, beginning a trend of single-digit black support for Republicans that has been sustained to the present moment.[51] If, in the Goldwater loss, we see a suggestion of the regional and racial realignment that characterizes contemporary party politics, by Nixon's presidency, the contours had clearly emerged.

In 1968, the politically supple Nixon abandoned the moderate rhetoric of his 1960 campaign and instead borrowed from Goldwater's conservative program, calling for a reform of the welfare state, pledging a strong national defense, using vigorous law and order rhetoric, and advocating states' rights. As Lee Edwards wrote, "[Goldwater's] articulation of private solutions to public problems laid the foundation for Nixon's appeal to the 'silent majority' in '68."[52] Because this represented a substantial shift in Nixon's campaign rhetoric, his campaign hired conservative staffers, such as Patrick Buchanan, and relied on the assistance of Goldwater's 1964 organization.[53] Starting as early as 1965, Goldwater also campaigned vigorously on Nixon's behalf, despite earlier misgivings about Nixon's conservative commitments.[54] These moves generally reassured the grassroots conservative movement, and they helped Nixon win where he did: the South and West.[55]

If Goldwater's conservatism was a "gut conservatism," Nixon's was a calculated conservatism. Goldwater's appeal in the West, and in the South in particular, was more fortuitous than it was conscious and strategic. Not so with Nixon, who was a "gut" politician.

Goldwater's principled commitment to limited national government made his stance on the racial politics of the time complicated. On the one hand, Goldwater was a strong proponent of federal government action to ensure voting rights for all Americans: "The right to vote is in the Constitution. There the federal government should act even if it means with troops," Goldwater said of black voting rights.[56] He voted for national civil rights legislation in the 1950s, and in his own state of Arizona, he promoted integration, including personally overseeing the integration of the Air National Guard units there and contributing money to an effort by the National Association for the Advancement of Colored People (NAACP) to challenge local school segregation.[57] Yet his rigid commitment to the Anti-Federalist constitutional reading of states' sovereignty made him unable to support the 1964 Civil Rights Act and national government–enforced desegregation.[58] Goldwater was not naïve. He knew that segregationists supported him, and he did not disavow them.[59] For him, a commitment to states' rights meant tolerating practices, like the segregation practiced by southern states, that he did not personally endorse. As he said of Governor Ross Barnett's 1962 refusal to allow James Meredith to enroll at the University of Mississippi, "While I feel the Governor was morally wrong in doing what he did, nevertheless, I feel he was within his Constitutional rights."[60] Despite Goldwater's efforts to explain his nuanced opposition to the 1964 Civil Rights Act (he supported some elements and was opposed to others on the grounds that they would create a "federal police force of mammoth proportions"), his vote against it firmly aligned him with southern Democrats and ultimately contributed to his victory in the states of the Deep South. The position on national government that Goldwater adopted as a conservative Westerner had strong appeal to white Southerners, and Goldwater accepted, if not tacitly encouraged, the electoral bounty that brought.[61]

Four years later, Nixon, who acknowledged that conservatives "don't like me but they tolerate me,"[62] actively sought to make himself more compelling to conservative voters in the South and West. He did not share Goldwater's instinctive suspicion of national government power, yet he learned from Goldwater's campaign the value of overtures to conservatives, and more importantly and specifically, the value of making appeals to white Southerners. In a more effortful and self-conscious attempt to build a Republican base in the South and to neutralize George Wallace's third party appeal, Nixon in 1968 assiduously courted white Southerners, making what David Broder called a "carefully planned circuit of the 11 states of the Confederacy."[63] Like Goldwater, Nixon, too, made an important political alliance with Strom Thurmond—for example, by telling a national reporter at a South Carolina press conference, "Strom is no racist. Strom is a man of courage and integrity."[64] While making it clear that he did not support segregation as part of the national Republican platform, Nixon echoed familiar states' rights concerns about Washington "dictating" local party policy and position.[65] Nixon even promised Thurmond and other southern reactionaries that in exchange for their support, he would curtail progress on civil rights.[66] In retrospect, Goldwater's public philosophy, and the South's opportunistic embrace of it, was the origin of the southern strategy that Nixon made famous.

The Republican strategy that eventually secured the South extended beyond advocating a slowdown on civil rights. What Nixon learned during his presidency, and what Reagan did instinctively, was to develop a broader suburban strategy with rhetoric that focused on issues of taxpayer rights, free enterprise, law and order to combat urban and campus unrest, strong national defense, and traditional social and religious beliefs.[67] This helped the party in suburbs nationwide beginning in the late 1960s, but especially in southern and western states with fast-growing, defense-related economies and fast-growing, suburban, middle-class communities. Distant from northeastern, Ivy-educated, elite power, believing themselves—often inaccurately, at least in the aggregate—to be government funders not beneficiaries, and interested in leading private lives freed from national governmental strictures, the new suburban voter responded to the conservative rhetoric first articulated nationally by Goldwater in 1964 and subsequently expanded and championed by Nixon and Reagan. This conservative rhetoric also provided a critical lens through which these predominantly white, middle-class voters could read the commitments of the New Deal state—and especially Johnson's War on Poverty extensions of it—in a new light.[68]

In short, a lot had changed in the South and West since 1964. Nixon and Reagan exploited these changes, adapting core components of Goldwater's public philosophy to these new circumstances. In doing so, they paid homage to Goldwater. In 1961, in his "Forgotten Americans" speech on the Senate floor, Goldwater had outlined conservative principles that would speak to the "forgotten" and "silent" Americans who "who quietly go about the business of paying and praying, working and saving." In his 1968 nomination acceptance speech, Nixon claimed that he would champion Goldwater's "forgotten Americans—the non-shouters, the non-demonstrators. They're not racists or sick;

they're not guilty of the crime that plagues the land. . . . They work in American factories, they run American businesses. They serve in government; they provide most of the soldiers who die to keep it free. They give drive to the spirit of America. They give lift to the American dream."[69]

More than the original southern strategy, Nixon's and Reagan's suburban strategy for the Republican Party was in accord with the conservative principles laid out by Goldwater. Yet part of what made the suburban strategy so successful was that it recalibrated and coded racial politics into conservative public philosophy. This was true on issues such as law and order (e.g., George Bush's Willie Horton ad), taxation and welfare state spending (e.g., "welfare queens"), and even on issues of morality (e.g., abortion funding and Christian schooling). While elaborating Goldwater's principles this way helped gain votes in regions that the 1964 campaign had demonstrated were receptive to Republicans, it warped Goldwater's conservative principles. In his later years, Goldwater publicly took issue with some of the directions of the new conservatism, breaking from the party on issues such as abortion, gays in the military, and campaign finance.[70]

In 1968, Nixon adapted Goldwater's conservative rhetoric for purely strategic and coalition-building reasons. Throughout the campaign, many conservatives remained distrustful of his commitment, and after he assumed the presidency, the concerns of these conservatives proved accurate. Worried more about being undermined by liberals, President Nixon pursued an expansion of the welfare state, greater regulation, new bureaucratic infrastructure, and improved relations with China and the Soviet Union.[71] These policies were all elaborations of the New Deal political order. As one scholar has written of Nixon and his actions as president: "He was no Goldwaterite."[72] Nixon's actions left conservatives such as Jesse Helms to bemoan that his "administration cannot escape a large measure of blame for the current easy acceptance of Leviathan-like government expansion.

This expansion has, if anything, become even faster under the current [Nixon] administration."[73]

Because Nixon feinted right and left (and because of Watergate), many analysts have described him as motivated by pure political ambition. While this may be true, it is also the case that Nixon presided in a crucial political moment in the developmental path of modern conservatism. The stinging repudiation of conservatism in 1964 was still fresh enough, and New Deal philosophy still vibrant enough, that to simply emulate Goldwater, in campaign and governance, would likely have been disastrous. At the same time, the very mechanisms of Goldwater's loss were also robust and beginning to bear fruit—his ideological critique of the New Deal, his organizational apparatus, and his "strategic" successes. These heralded a new world not yet fully there in 1968.

To the extent that Nixon fed both the "Leviathan-like government expansion" and the conservative critique of the modern state, he hastened conservatives' triumph in 1980. The rise of new economic powerhouses abroad, stagflation at home, new rounds of urban crisis, and turmoil in the Middle East contributed to Americans' sense of unease with New Deal solutions in the 1970s. Goldwater had tried to change the terms of political debate in 1964, and the country was not ready. By 1980, it was. As the man whose political star was first burnished when he made his "A Time for Choosing" speech on behalf of Goldwater, Ronald Reagan was the logical successor to bring Goldwater's conservative legacy to full maturation. He was able to do this because of the groundwork Goldwater laid and that Nixon had paradoxically deepened.

Consider three developments that occurred immediately upon Reagan's election. First, his inaugural address echoed the public philosophy of Goldwater, and now was endorsed by the new majority that would prevail at least until 2008: government is not the solution to the problem, it is the problem. Second, echoing Goldwater's tough foreign policy stance, Reagan blamed the Iranian hostage crisis on President Carter's "weakness and vacillation," and his willingness to negotiate (or engage in "appeasement") with the Ayatollah.[74] The public broadly applauded his strong, militaristic foreign policy stance, and Reagan's resurrection of an arms race fight against communism was vindicated by the ultimate collapse of the Soviet Union.[75] Third, Reagan channeled Goldwater again when, in his first year in office and despite a 1980 campaign endorsement from the Professional Air Traffic Controllers Organization (one of the few unions to back Reagan), he fired 12,000 of the striking union workers, setting a tone for labor/management relations markedly different from that of the New Deal and one that continues to the present. It was also a change from President Nixon, who oversaw public sector union growth on parallel with the industrial union growth of the 1930s.[76] In the decades following Reagan's tough stance, the number of strikes and union membership both decreased significantly.

In these three vignettes, which set the tone for Reagan's presidency, we can see how Goldwater's vision was finally, fully realized. Like Nixon, Reagan had campaigned on conservative themes: law and order, strong defense, limited national government, and states' rights.[77] Like Nixon, he was rewarded with increased Republican support nationwide, but especially in the South and West. Like Nixon, there was strategic gain to be had in advancing these themes—the support of an alienated white middle and working class often living in suburbs, the support of those dependent on the defense industry, and the support of those unnerved by social change. Unlike Nixon, however, Reagan was closer to a true conservative. His "revolution" followed through on the rhetoric by seeking to enact conservative policies, including a rollback of the welfare state, reduced taxation, increased defense, and changed labor/management relations.

Reagan's success in linking rhetoric to policy and strategy to belief is evidence of Goldwater's ultimate victory. Goldwater failed in 1964 because he refused to be positioned within the existing terms of political contest (which ran from New Deal–extension to New Deal–light). But this refusal put in place a new frame of reference, one that would be cultivated by subsequent Republican leaders so successfully that in a mere sixteen years, a majority of voters were endorsing the same principles they had only recently found foreign and "extreme."

"He's Going to Run as Barry Goldwater"

Near the end of the primary campaign, Goldwater went to Georgia to shore up his support among at-large delegates. At one stop, he had to be prompted to address an adoring crowd. As Rick Perlstein describes: "A reporter poked a microphone in his snoot; Goldwater scowled. A pretty young thing tried to plop a big white cowboy hat on his head; he shoved her away. A guy was peddling a canned soft drink . . . 'Gold Water' ('The Right Drink for the Conservative Taste') from the tailgate of his truck. Goldwater was offered a sip. He spit it out. 'This tastes like piss! I wouldn't drink it with gin!'"[78]

Irascible, intemperate, irreverent, Goldwater was hardly the candidate with a personality suited for a national political campaign. Indeed, these very traits contributed to his defeat by giving credence to the caricatures of his substantive views as extreme and unpredictable. They provided the perfect fodder for LBJ's campaign to launch a program of attack ads (including the infamous "Daisy" ad) unlike any seen before.[79] At the same time, as one recent account explains, Goldwater was "an exemplar of civility, decency, and integrity," even according to those opposed to his political views. Robert Kennedy Jr. described Goldwater as "neither mean-spirited nor racist" but someone who challenged liberals with "sensible argument and honest conviction."[80] Irascible but not mean-spirited. Intemperate but civil. Goldwater was capable of not giving offense but he was a straight shooter, and as a candidate, he chose not to curb his personality simply to curry favor with voters or the media. While dooming his presidential candidacy, these very qualities of temperament and character help account for Goldwater's crucial role in founding the modern conservative reconstruction of American politics.

Prompted by handlers to trim his opinions, or to reach out to constituencies, or to appear more likable, Goldwater refused or at least failed to follow a game plan that was designed to make his candidacy more broadly appealing. At the beginning of the general campaign, observers expressed shock when it became clear that he would "run as Barry Goldwater."[81] He refused even to change his campaign slogan—"In your heart, you know he's right," a damning slogan if there ever was one—despite it being the least favorably received of five slogans pretested by his campaign.[82] In its recognition of the long odds for electoral success, this slogan candidly captured the challenge and the significance of Goldwater's leadership. Who chooses a campaign slogan that seems more of an announcement of a forthcoming loss than of victory's rallying cry? Goldwater was tapping something incipient, something that people were not yet ready to acknowledge. In labeling it, making it his campaign slogan, he began the process of making public and acceptable that which had been hidden and unspoken. Unlike the model of a rational politician, whose primary object is to win position and power by deploying ideas, strategies, and public personas as instruments, Goldwater used the occasion of his own electoral campaign as the instrument to facilitate the success of a coherent new public philosophy. His temperament—including his honest conviction and his integrity—was perfectly suited to this project.

Goldwater was not oblivious to the requirements of modern campaigning. He had, after all, been successful in winning office as a senator.[83] Throughout the 1964 campaign, he took seriously the need for fund-raising and ensuring support from delegates. What made his commitment to these endeavors distinct from that of other politicians, however, is that he saw them as tools necessary to advance his conservative ideas rather than as tools merely to advance his electoral ambitions. Indeed, much of his initial reluctance to stand as a candidate for the Republican nomination was because he wanted to make a credible enough showing so as not to undermine his conservative project.

Because Goldwater was the most viable and credible conservative candidate for the presidency, a diverse set of efforts was undertaken to persuade him or to draft him to run, as described earlier. Goldwater was always wary that these draft movements had agendas different from his own. His own agenda had more to do with the viability of the conservative project than mere electability. Thus, to win election at the cost of modifying his ideas was unacceptable. When his supporters sought to refashion his campaign using the standard tricks of the trade to make him more appealing as a national candidate, Goldwater was offended. For example, he resisted attempts to highlight politically attractive attributes of his biography—that he was a ham radio operator, that he was a licensed pilot, that he had served in the military, that he was a member of the NAACP, and that he personally organized relief flights for starving Navajo families during his time in the Army Air Corps reserves.[84] He resisted any attempts to turn his campaign into a cult of personality, which would supplant a central focus on the new public philosophy he was promoting.

He was similarly offended by his handlers' efforts to modify his views to make them more broadly palatable. When Republicans and Democrats alike called him an extremist, rather than changing his positions on the central policy issues of the time he responded vigorously—including saying famously in his nomination acceptance speech, "I would remind you that extremism in the defense of liberty is no vice. And let me remind you also that moderation in the pursuit of justice is no virtue."

While this defense was similar to sentiments expressed by esteemed American political actors ranging from the framers to Martin Luther King Jr., high-profile opponents—including Martin Luther King Jr. and Senator William Fulbright—and even media outlets responded by likening his campaign and ideas to "Hitlerism" and "Russian Stalinism."[85] Yet in the face of such damning remarks about his campaign, Goldwater chose not to tailor his views to the understandings of the moderate center.

Rather, he sought to reeducate that center about the deficiencies of a view that privileged adjectives, like extreme and moderate, over nouns, like liberty and justice.

Of course, Goldwater's impatience and irascibility was sometimes an instinctive attribute of his personality and not a principled decision on his part. This hurt his candidacy and frustrated his handlers. Nevertheless, these qualities of character fit well with the sort of campaign that he preferred and fit poorly with traditional political campaigns that are, understandably, designed to win power and influence for the candidate.

Unable to sacrifice his integrity and unwilling to glad-hand like a typical politician, Barry Goldwater behaved during his campaign in ways that contributed to his loss. Yet his uncompromising attitude preserved intact his conservative political philosophy, the conservative organization, and Republican political strategy. Consider the following counterfactuals. Imagine that in the face of Johnson's critique of Goldwater as a warmonger, Goldwater had changed his position to prioritize diplomacy over threats of military coercion in order to achieve peace. Imagine that in the face of criticism that he was a racist, Goldwater had endorsed more aggressive federal measures to advance the desegregation goals that he, in fact, favored. Imagine that he had allowed his campaign operatives to refocus the campaign on these new positions, linking them to his attractive biography.

It is plausible, if not likely, that the election results would have been closer, and this would have meant that his campaign would have been viewed as more competent and that he would have remained—and may have been enhanced—in his status as leader of the Republican Party. But the cost would have been that the party that he would have nominally led was the same one he was trying to reform. The new organizations that had worked to nominate him would either have been disaffected or coopted. He would have been no different from Rockefeller or Nixon. His party would have been their party. And indeed, in 1968 and beyond, the question for the party would have been, who would be the best "Rockefeller" or "Nixon"—that is, who would be the best Republican version of the New Deal?

Instead, Goldwater refused to allow either his candidacy or conservatism to be diluted. By preserving his integrity and maintaining the meaning of the conservative cause, Goldwater altered the developmental path of the Republican Party and ultimately the nation. According to conventional wisdom, Reagan was able to accomplish what Goldwater could not because of his genial personality. Neglected in this proverbial wisdom is that Goldwater's personality was critical to establishing and preserving the predicates of Reagan's own election.

The Political Significance of Integrity

Because of the success of modern conservatism, Goldwater has enjoyed renewed political attention and significant scholarly interest. He is seen as a man ahead of his time. He expressed ideas before they were acceptable and therefore can be instructive to people today who want to recover the original versions of today's reigning public philosophy. As scholars revisited the Goldwater campaign, they discovered that his effort provided a remarkable window through which to view and reinterpret an entire political era. Previously thought to be a time of liberal dominance and progressive, even radical, resurgence, the 1960s are now seen by scholars as a time of fractures and substrata, leading to publications such as *The Conservative Sixties*.[86] In these returns to Goldwater, civic or scholarly, the emphasis is on Goldwater as a marker for a time, important for what he represented, not for what he did. Indeed, some scholars see his massive political loss as a setback for a future conservative reconstruction of American politics.

Goldwater's loss was not a setback for the modern conservative movement. The other elements of the conventional wisdom are not wrong—there is much truth in them. But they miss the most important point. Our central thesis is that Goldwater was remarkably important for what he did and said, not just for what he symbolized. We have tried to show how the very elements that contributed to his massive political defeat in 1964 facilitated the rapid reformation of the American political order.

In 1964, William Buckley told young Goldwaterites to prepare for defeat as Goldwater's nomination came "before we had time properly to prepare the ground," but that his candidacy would plant "seeds of hope, which will flower on a great November day in the future."[87] Goldwater was not just ahead of his time and he did far more than simply "plant seeds of hope." Both characterizations suggest a passivity that we challenge, a passivity often attributed to losers. Were he ahead of his time, that would suggest a radical disjunction between the actions of a leader and the movements of history. This is an understandable conclusion for observers of his massive political loss because loss suggests that he was not really a leader at all but rather, a failed leader, a loser.

We have tried to show how the very factors that led to massive political defeat in 1964—an alien public philosophy, a nonmainstream campaign organization, an undeveloped political strategy, and a political character and temperament ill-suited to a national campaign—all contributed to the success of the revolt against the New Deal constitutional moment, what might be more generally understood as the Reagan antimoment. We see these attributes of Goldwater's loss and ultimate success as features that developed out of his practice of political integrity, as opposed to the practices of a traditional politician. In doing so, we underscore Goldwater's agency as a political actor. In each instance—promulgating political views, organizing, strategizing, and campaigning—Goldwater made a choice to act as he did. The reaction that his actions generated consolidated conservatism as the dominant political mode of the future. And it may be that Goldwater understood the possibilities that he unleashed. Reflecting on Goldwater's moniker, "the cheerful malcontent," George Will writes: "It takes a rare and fine temperament to wed that adjective with that noun. His emotional equipoise was undisturbed by the loss of 44 states as a presidential nominee. Perhaps he sensed that he had won the future."[88]

While it is our contention that he did win, his success was compromised. The success of conservatism is self-evident in the dominance of the public philosophy of "limited government" even today, as well as in policy achievements, the rightward turn in two-party politics, and the electoral victories of conservative Republicans. Nonetheless, the very same Republican Party that electorally profited from Goldwater's actions has promoted views at odds with his definition of conservatism (a libertarian conservatism). On issues ranging from abortion to gay rights, Goldwater broke ranks with the modern Republican Party when it used its success to pursue socially conservative policies that impinged upon individual liberty. Modern conservative leaders, like Paul Ryan, invoke Goldwater while simultaneously denying parts of his conservative vision. Seeking the 2012 Republican nomination, Ryan paid tribute to Goldwater when he told conservative supporters, "Americans deserve a choice—a choice between two dramatically different visions for our country's future"; yet Ryan repudiated him by including as part of the conservative choice a commitment to upholding "traditional family and community values"—the buzzwords of social conservatism.[89]

Goldwater's integrity enabled modern conservatism to flourish, and this is its political significance. Because he lost authorship of conservatism to subsequent politicians, his integrity also led him to forswear key elements of the very success he created. And while he was critical of the way Republican politicians damaged conservatism as he understood it, Goldwater nonetheless bears some responsibility for this development as it was his leadership had facilitated their ability to do so with such success. This, too, is politically significant.

5

Legacies of Loss in
American Politics

The Anti-Federalists' opposition to the ratification of the Constitution, Andrew Johnson's resistance to Reconstruction, and Barry Goldwater's repudiation of the New Deal are all extraordinarily successful counterpoints to the decisive regime shaping victories in American political history. For each so-called constitutional moment, there has been a powerful "antimoment" of profound significance for American political development. In each case, the initial political loss is massive and undeniable and, nevertheless, in each case the political objectives of the loser are advanced in the long run. These outcomes, which run counter to standard narratives of American history, are interesting and important for that brute fact—that losing programs and ideas are not total losses and, correspondingly, massive political and constitutional victories are not as successful as usually presumed. More important, and even more counterintuitive, the losers' eventual successes are tightly connected to the mechanisms of loss. In other words, the very same reasons, choices, and alleged missteps that account for the initial loss are instruments for the later, long-term success of each "antimoment."

The connection of the mechanisms of loss to later success suggests that learning how to lose a political contest can be as important as learning how to win. Traditional narratives of American politics—of victory and loss—obscure this. Importantly, in each of our cases, conventional understandings of what it meant to win or lose prevented most observers, at the time and afterward, from seeing the opportunities that were created and sustained by the losers. When the losers' political heirs subsequently exploited these opportunities, the resulting victories have been either misunderstood or underappreciated. Only by recognizing that the losers have agency—by seeing them not as passive and vanquished victims but as political actors with strategies of their own and capable of creating legacies of their own—can we begin to appreciate their impress on American politics.

Taken together, our three antimoments illustrate the importance of treating losing itself as a potential source of agency in politics. However, the mechanisms of loss differed in each case, and they reveal a variety of ways that losing may transform itself into success. Before we elaborate how these self-transforming defeats recast our understanding of major synoptic accounts of American politics, a review of the variety of overlooked mechanisms at work in these cases is in order.

Sometimes the act of losing is profoundly strategic. Andrew Johnson is our most obvious case of a strategic loser. Losers who make purposeful choices contrary to traditional prescriptions for what it means to "lead successfully" possess an acute understanding of the challenging context they face. Finding himself a southern president of the North in the aftermath of the Civil War, Andrew Johnson's ambitions were contrary to those of the country he led. His cognizance of this fact compelled him to immediately adopt new strategies—the strategies of the dispossessed—to achieve his aims. Knowing he could not persuade Radicals in Congress and citizens of the North, more generally, to enact his Restoration plan, he sought to achieve it through other means. His aim became to obstruct the Radical Republican agenda by thwarting their initiatives.

As we discussed in chapter 3, Johnson deployed tactics of

delay, misinformation, and presidential vetoes and executive orders to obstruct the Reconstruction agenda. He acted pre-emptively on the claimed authority of the presidency (drawing upon a robust reading of the Federalists' sophisticated version of executive power). And he constructed ideological, political, and logistic space for the South to begin rebuilding based on an Anti-Federalist reading of the Constitution. These acts formed a self-conscious strategy that was celebrated in the South and decried in the North. These efforts were necessary for him to begin, and for others to complete, the task of restoring the South to the Union on the racial and economic order grounds it pre-ferred. This was a remarkable achievement that upends our or-dinary understanding of leadership today. Consider, for example, this headline for a story reacting to the early candidacy in 2015 of Senator Ted Cruz for president of the United States. "Can the Obstructionist in Chief Become Commander in Chief?"[1] Although Ted Cruz lost to Donald Trump in the contest for the Republican nomination, Andrew Johnson shows that it is possible for obstruction to be an instrument of leadership and change. One cannot simply assume that obstruction and lead-ership are antithetical. Moreover, Cruz's obstructionism along with the larger obstructionist strategy of his Republican party, beginning with the election of President Obama in 2008, may have legitimized Donald Trump's unprecedented, unorthodox, and uncivil leadership style. For Johnson, obstruction was an in-strument of strategic leadership. Thus, one might say Johnson repudiated *leadership* in its traditional form.

Like Andrew Johnson, Barry Goldwater had an acute under-standing of the challenging context he faced. However, Gold-water's agency was not strategic in the same way. His instru-ment to achieve the outcomes he sought was his integrity as a person and the coherence and intellectual integrity of his ideol-ogy. By integrity we do not mean that his personality was ap-pealing or that his ideology was persuasive or fully defensible from an impartial point of view. As we mention in chapter 4, Goldwater could be an irascible and unpleasant man (though often, as many have noted, he could also be decent and appealing). And his views were partisan and therefore less than fully persuasive from an impartial point of view (as would be those of his most articulate and thoughtful opponents on the left). By integrity, we mean to suggest that Goldwater held to a consistent view of his constitutional duties, to a consistent understanding of the Constitution, and to a consistent partisan program *that he refused to adulterate for personal political advantage.* As a senator, he was able to respect his opponents and to compromise without abandoning any core principles, and as a presidential candidate, he was eager to engage his opponents on the plane of ideas and reasons rather than on the terrain of passions and demagogic manipulations.[2]

Because Lyndon Johnson's campaign was so successful in demonizing Barry Goldwater by raising fears of the prospect of a Goldwater presidency, during the 2016 campaign many journalists analogized Donald Trump to Barry Goldwater. Such comparisons are woefully wrong and inapt. While both politicians challenged the party establishment and appealed to far-right elements within the Republican Party, there is no ideological core to Trump personally, no movement independent of his personal appeal, and no integrity that marks his conduct as a leader. Most significantly, Trump successfully won through genuinely norm-busting demagogic appeals, while Goldwater lost partly due to the skillful demagogy of LBJ's campaign. For Donald Trump, the more accurate analogy is Andrew Johnson, the only true demagogue to previously ascend to the office of president of the United States. Johnson was eventually impeached for behavior similar to Trump's (though the specific charge of inflammatory rhetoric was dropped as the impeachment case moved from the House to the Senate). These reflections were prompted by the initial consensus that Trump was likely to lose the election, so it was natural to compare him to previous losers. However, his electoral victory might be better understood as an unfortunate legacy of the losses we have described, including Barry Goldwater's.

In *some* ways, Goldwater resembles other politicians today

who are deemed "purists" for their uncompromising attachment to ideology. When the price of winning is a candidate elected to office willing to accommodate, logroll, and compromise—in short, to behave like a politician—purists would prefer the loss. Loss under these circumstances is a victory for the purist because it keeps the ideology unsullied. For the typical purist, political victory on compromised terms would be a defeat, so political defeat with ideology intact is a kind of victory. However, the typical purist's personal "victory" remains a political defeat to the extent that no political change, in the short or long term, is led or even incubated.

Many have seen the significance of Barry Goldwater's 1964 electoral defeat in precisely these terms. While Goldwater may be a typical purist in some respects, he is more interesting as an example of an *atypical* purist—one who was able to wield his commitments in a way that resulted in significant, long-term influence and change. Most purists simply fail in electoral politics. Goldwater is a purist who turned failure into success. Whereas Andrew Johnson repudiated leadership in its traditional form, Goldwater repudiated *politics* in its traditional form.

Because Goldwater's mechanism for his success was to repudiate politics in its traditional form, most observers don't understand that he was nonetheless an agent of the eventual success of conservatism. He is often referred to, mistakenly in our view, as a man ahead of his times—someone who could have been a successful "change agent" had he come along a little later. As we explained in chapter 4, rather than seeing Goldwater in a missed moment, we see the very actions that he took, which doomed him in 1964, as critical to facilitating the eventual success of conservatism. It was his refusal to change his posture, his policies, or his personality that preserved and inspired conservatism at the late heights of the New Deal era, giving it the jump-start it needed to become a politically viable popular movement.

The Andrew Johnson case demonstrates that skillful and creative leadership may be deeply problematic. It may frustrate the deeper aspirations of democracy or, depending on one's understanding of democracy, it may advance democracy at the expense of other constitutional values. The concepts of entrepreneurship and leadership, now in vogue in political science and popular discourse, can be too narrow to capture the political direction of change because they purport to be neutral or value free. These terms are better discussed in tandem with a notion like statesmanship, because taken together, the terms can elucidate the content and direction of the change being sought as well as the strategy and tactics deployed.[3] Johnson was an exceptionally effective leader. But in considering what he accomplished, we realize that the more effective he was as a leader, the more he failed as a statesman.

Our account of the legacy of Johnson's loss uncovers and illustrates a design flaw in the logic of the functioning of American constitutionalism. Much like a hacker whose virus exploits the operating system of a computer, Andrew Johnson exploited and successfully subverted a basic attribute of the constitutional order. In the understanding of *The Federalist*, for example, the Constitution will be effective to the extent that it is able to institutionalize hypocrisy. Political self-interest is translated into action for the common good by the creation of incentives for ambitious politicians to defend their actions with publicly justifiable reasons. In this view, the injustice or prejudice of individual motives becomes politically irrelevant to the extent that politicians feel constrained to justify their actions with good reasons—through reasons that may not have actually been their motivation. As long as politics trades on the plane of these public-regarding rationalizations, liberal constitutionalism will have worked.

Now one might have thought that this attribute of American politics would have precluded manifestly unjust policies like those that paid little heed to the needs of former slaves or those that continued to perpetuate the ills of racism. Even if racist and unjust motivations compelled a particular politician's policy pursuits, he would have to mask that in public with good language sufficiently persuasive, on its merits, to compel support from other politicians with other interests and constituencies to whom they must answer. But the circumstances of constitutional failure surrounding the Civil War forced those who would rid the Constitution of slavery to adopt means and arguments that went beyond the Constitution. Thus, Radical Republicans imposed a settlement on the South, violated the terms for amending the document, adopted military tribunals in the place of civil courts, and more generally, allowed abstract notions of justice to trump settled legal practice—they, in other words, acted against the dictates of the Constitution. Yet most important, the partisans of the northern vision of Reconstruction argued that all these policies were legitimate *because they were constitutional.* Few, if any, Republicans argued that necessity required extraconstitutional emergency measures for Reconstruction. They pretended to operate under a constitution, while they actually operated outside it. In this circumstance, the logic of constitutional hypocrisy might not work as intended. Andrew Johnson was thus sometimes able to construct better constitutional arguments than his opponents could, even while pursuing ends at odds with constitutional liberalism. Johnson covered his narrow and unjust sectionalist motives with plausible, sometimes sound constitutional argument, whereas his opponents distorted the Constitution, however sound their political motives. By exploiting the logic of constitutionally induced argument, Andrew Johnson succeeded as a leader while failing as a statesman. In doing so, he reveals a limit of the political architecture—a point at which the Constitution fails.

Over the long term, Barry Goldwater proved an exceptionally successful leader. The jury is still out, however, on history's ultimate judgment of Goldwater as a statesman. A growing literature is highlighting the virtues of his character as well as the relative moderation and intelligence of his policies compared to many post-Reagan conservatives. His ability to compromise while still maintaining a principled position and his civility toward his ideological adversaries also made him an unusually responsible partisan. Yet even well-defended policies, policies advanced with integrity, can still be seriously mistaken. In Goldwater's case, for example, his vote against the 1964 Civil Rights Act was a serious mistake. As we explained in detail, Goldwater had a more nuanced stance on how to advance civil rights than is generally allowed, and over the course of his career, he more consistently advocated civil rights than did some of the most famous white politicians of the time. But his concern that federal action could sometimes exacerbate problems of discrimination rather than ameliorate them and his constitutional objection to federal intrusions on state authority led him to oppose the 1964 act. Ultimately, Goldwater proved to be very wrong about the character of the law and its enforcement over time. He also provided political and intellectual resources for racists who became attracted to him, to his movement, and to the misuse of his ideology. If Andrew Johnson reminds us that effective leadership is not the same thing as statesmanship, Goldwater reminds us that statesmanship requires more than leadership with integrity.

The Anti-Federalists present a very different picture of political agency. The art of appropriation that we discussed in chapter 2 can also be described as a sequence and interaction of two forms of agency. The Anti-Federalists' initial action is reactive—a response to the Federalist proposal for a new regime. The initial reaction was a hard-hitting and very frank critique of the Federalist proposal, one that depicted the Constitution as a dramatic change of the status quo. It was designed to persuade and to defeat. This initial set of actions generated a reaction from the Federalist side, which was difficult to predict in advance.[4] The second instance of agency is the exploitation of the Federalist response. The Anti-Federalists pivoted from condemnation of the Constitution and its proponents during ratification to appropriation of the authority of the victors once the new regime was established. Anti-Federalist success derived from their actions but even more importantly from what their actions prompted the Federalists to do. The difficulty and improbability of ratification of the new Constitution forced Federalists to respond directly to the Anti-Federalists' clear articulation of the portent of the proposed constitution. It is the Federalist response that facilitated eventual Anti-Federalist success, and were it not for the initial charges levied by the Anti-Federalists, the tools for subsequent appropriation by Anti-Federal intellectual heirs would not have been present.

The Federalist response made them the unwitting abettors of the long-term Anti-Federalist victory. Sometimes the conventional "winners" provide tools, by the fact of their win or how they win, for the losers to reconstitute their loss into success. Thus, a more complicated notion of agency attends the first constitutional juncture in the history of the American regime than is exhibited in the two subsequent crises. This is perhaps fitting because the three constitutional junctures are not equivalent "constitutional moments" as is sometimes thought. Subsequent constitutional crises operate under the umbrella of the ratification debate, revisiting, appropriating, and deploying contending political ideas generated at the Founding. Although the surprisingly potent long-term influence of the Anti-Federalists muted the presumed victory of America's Federalist founders, it also reveals that America's first constitutional moment was its only genuine episode of regime constitution. While undoubtedly unusually significant and transformative of political practices on the ground, Reconstruction/Restoration in the mid-nineteenth century and the New Deal/Reagan Revolution today formed under the auspices of and with political and rhetorical resources provided by the founding Federal/Anti-Federal debate.

Constitution and Reconstitution

Among the most important and insightful accounts of American politics are those that seek to map and understand the three pivotal eras and moments of crucial change in American history. As we mentioned in chapter 1, the most well-known studies of this type are the pathbreaking writings by Theodore Lowi, Walter Dean Burnham, and Bruce Ackerman. All of these authors agree with each other on the basic character of these junctures and how to understand their meaning. All mark the founding of the Constitution, the Civil War and Reconstruction, and the New Deal as moments of pivotal change and constitutive significance. All see the results of political contests at each juncture as a rout for the party that prevails, a victory so thoroughgoing and total that the loser comes to accept the political ideals and political language of the victor. All of these leading thinkers understand the three episodes as politically equivalent, that is, as successive regimes. No one is more significant than the rest. Lowi's successive American "republics," Burnham's "critical elections," and Ackerman's "constitutional moments" all share these basic understandings.

Our study of the neglected antimoments at each of these junctures calls into question, or seriously qualifies, most of these verities that form the conventional wisdom. To be sure, the three constitutional junctures are moments of pivotal change. The first element of the conventional wisdom, that the Founding, Reconstruction, and New Deal were eras of profound change is certainly true. However, these constitutional moments are not equal in constitutive significance. Only the first is a true regime change. And none of the three "moments" mark victories as total or thoroughgoing as is usually thought. Because of this, the second two constitutional moments operate under the auspices of the unresolved first and redeploy and elaborate resources provided in the original contest.

Each constitutional juncture did mark a profound change from the way politics was practiced and experienced in the previous era. Before the Civil War, slavery was legal in the South and afterward it was not. Before the New Deal, the role of the national government in regulating the economy and providing social benefits was minimal. After the New Deal, the modern administrative state was born and became a permanent attribute of American political and social life. Yet, as important as changes on the ground are to the lives of those who experience them, they only reflect true *regime* changes if the economic and social needs that drove and justified them are disconnected from the Constitution as a work of political architecture. The assumption that drives the notion that America is marked by successive regimes, or constitutionally equivalent transformations, is the idea that the Constitution is only an arrangement of offices and powers—the instruments of governance—and that it leaves the economic, social, and cultural spheres to a world outside of the Constitution and outside of politics. Sometimes this premise is expressed in the commonplace that the Constitution was made for an eighteenth-century world that no longer exists and needs to be updated for the nineteenth, twentieth, or twenty-first centuries.[5] Modern liberals articulate a version of this when, for example, they rail against the Constitution for legalizing slavery. When modern conservatives argue for a return to the "original" meaning of the Constitution with regard to the size of the federal government or the power of the states, they, too, operate on this premise.

This familiar and conventional view is an inheritance of the Anti-Federal appropriation that we detailed in chapter 2. The notion that the original Constitution was principally a legal document, that its meaning was tethered to the extant practices of the time in which it was written, and that the subsequent growth of federal power, size of government, and extent of national responsibilities are revolutionary departures from this original compact is the revisionist view of the *losers* in the debate over the founding of the Constitution. As we discussed in chapter 2, this losers' view was constructed to achieve through interpretation what was lost in constitutional construction. The Anti-Federalists preferred the Articles of Confederation to the Constitution, so when they lost, they and their heirs successfully appropriated early iterations of *The Federalist* to interpret the Constitution as a less nationalist project than it was, and also a more *legalistic* project than it was.

Indeed, before those losers—the Anti-Federalists—actually lost, when they were opponents in a contest that had not yet been decided, they emphasized even more strongly than the Federalists that the Constitution was a political design for a large commercial republic where national power would increase dramatically over time. In chapter 2 we stressed that this shared understanding of the projected working of the polity designed by the Constitution—what we called its *political* logic—is the core of the meaning of the Constitution and of the victory of its supporters. This central fact in the making of the American polity is missed by some of the major scholars of American political development.

Consider Theodore Lowi's striking contrast between the Founding and New Deal constitutional orders. Beginning with the premise that the Constitution provides the national government with only expressly delegated powers, reserving all others to the states, Lowi derives a list of domestic national responsibilities from the list of legislative powers adumbrated in Article I. He constructs a representative list of other governmental functions that remain with the states. Thus, the federal government is confined to internal improvements, subsidies, tariffs, public lands disposal, patents, and coinage. The states, on the other hand, have custody of property laws, estate and inheritance laws, commerce and contracts, banking and credit laws, insurance law, family law, morals law, education law, public health and quarantine, general penal laws, public works, land use law, water and mineral resource law, electoral law, local government law, civil service law, occupations and professions law, and more. As a general description of American political life in the nineteenth century, these lists do indeed capture domestic political life as it was experienced.[6]

Yet there are a number of problems with this depiction. First, restricting the enumeration of legitimate national activity to Article I of the Constitution, the legislative article, ignores the instruction within the article to look beyond it, "to make all Laws which shall be necessary and proper for carrying into Execution the foregoing powers, and all other Powers vested by this Constitution in the Government of the United States, or in any Department of Officer thereof." Second, Lowi asserts that the Constitution only contains expressly granted powers, contrary to the core understandings of Federalists and Anti-Federalists as we discussed in chapter 2. Finally, Lowi asserts that the original

Constitution made "state laws more fundamental than the national laws." For him, the New Deal marks a fundamental transformation because "for the first time the national government established a direct and coercive relationship between itself and individual citizens."[7] If that proposition were true, the New Deal would indeed be a regime change. But it is false.[8]

During the ratification debate, the Anti-Federalists and the Federalists alike urged interpretations opposed to the very points Lowi highlights. The Necessary and Proper Clause was thought to portend an expanding central state; implied powers were shown to be necessary features of the new Constitution and were thus attacked by the Anti-Federalists and defended by the Federalists; and most significantly, the crux of the dispute over ratification was precisely that the new Constitution established for the first time a direct, unmediated, and coercive relationship between the central government and ordinary citizens. Under the Articles of Confederation that relationship was constitutive of state sovereignty. The new Constitution upended that principle. It is this fundamental change that fueled the Anti-Federal opposition to the proposed Constitution and it is this feature that the Federalists thought most necessary.

The central dispute between the Federalists and Anti-Federalists concerned precisely the proposition that Lowi ascribes, instead, to the New Deal. The decisive change from the Articles of Confederation to the Constitution was the establishment of a direct and coercive relationship between the federal government and individual citizens. There is simply no doubt that this principle was established by the ratification of the Constitution. It is of course true that the federal government did not use all the power available to it until social and economic circumstances prompted calls for its use. But even that fact was fully appreciated by both sides in the original founding debate. When the Anti-Federalists railed against what some today would call "big government," it was an image of that *future* that motivated their campaign. It was a future predicted on the basis of fundamental choices that the Constitution inscribed, including the commitments to governance of a huge polity rather than to a league of small nations. And the iterations of *The Federalist* were designed to persuade citizens that such a future was not to be feared but in fact was desirable. In chapter 2, we described this shared founding understanding as the "political logic" of the Constitution.

Ackerman and Burnham do not repeat, or necessarily agree with, all of Lowi's particulars regarding the junctures of regime change. But each reveals similar understandings of the meaning of the Constitution and the logic of change. For example, like Lowi, Burnham sees the Constitution as an arrangement of offices and powers suitable for the nineteenth century, but out of date today. He views the document as a palimpsest that is rewritten and remade for unanticipated social and economic circumstances. Ackerman takes issue with the professional narrative of legal academics who justify the Civil War amendments and the New Deal as elaborations of the original Constitution. Thus, Lowi, Burnham, and Ackerman all treat the Constitution as a legal document whose original meaning is tethered to the institutions and practices of the time in which it was written. All treat constitutional provisions, arrangements and understandings as reactions to socioeconomic development rather than as a constitutive cause of those very developments. Again, as we showed in chapter 2, the more cramped legalistic and reactive view was not the understanding of proponents and opponents of the Constitution during the ratification campaign. Rather, the Constitution was a plan for the future and an expression of fundamental political choices that helped bring that future into being. At stake, in other words, were the core commitments of this new design and their social, institutional, cultural, and policy implications. From that founding perspective, the Constitution would not be a "living document" whose meaning needed to be changed to accommodate unknown and unanticipated economic and social developments but rather would itself set in motion a polity that would generate such economic and social change as a necessary consequence of the basic choices the Constitution represented. Those generated problems would justify the use of national power that the Constitution had provided from the time of ratification. Again, this is what we described as the political logic of the Constitution.

We do not mean to argue that all the policies of Reconstruction and later the Progressive and New Deal eras occurred inevitably or that all agencies, programs, and regulations developed in the cause of "big government" were constitutional. For one thing, there is no single strand of policies that marks these eras—as we have shown. Many policies contradicted one another. More important, our argument regarding the political logic of the Constitution cannot readily yield judgments regarding the wisdom or constitutionality of particular policies at particular times. Our broad claim, that there is a political logic at the heart of our forward-looking Founding, cannot account for the precise timing or character of the political institutions and practices that were later developed. For that, one would be well advised to turn to the rich and growing literature in political science that details the historically particular ways institutional change is negotiated against prior inherited institutions and practices. But our account is sufficient, we think, to show that American political development has a constitutionally induced direction. Whether ordinary citizens fully understood this at the time, the ratification debate between the most intelligent protagonists shows that adoption of the Constitution would commit them to a national government, a national economy, a largely commercial way of life, a strong executive, and a judiciary with wide interpretative license long before the necessity of those attributes for our polity became fully manifest. They became manifest because of social, cultural, and economic developments that the fundamental design commitments set in motion.[9]

The shift of legitimate authority from a broad regime building understanding of *constitution making* to a legalist understanding of *constitutional interpretation* is one of the supreme triumphs of the Anti-Federalist movement after it lost the ratification debate. One of the ironies revealed in the conventional wisdom of political science today is that the work of these scholars is further evidence of the success of the Anti-Federal appropriation. Not only conservative justices, like Antonin Scalia and Clarence Thomas, but also progressive thinkers, like Burnham and Ackerman, evidence the continuing victory of the defeated Anti-Federal movement. One of the most interesting legacies of loss in American politics is the conceptual framework of major scholars of regime change in American political development. The idea that under the original Constitution the federal government is limited to enumerated powers, the claim that the ratified central government did not have coercive authority over individual citizens, and the legalistic mode of constitutional interpretation can only be supported by early iterations of the Federalist response to the Anti-Federal critique. That rhetoric was exploited by the Anti-Federalist losers in their attempts to alter, if not subvert, the trajectory of American politics. During the ratification itself, the Anti-Federalists predicted and the Federalists eventually defended precisely the contours of a polity that conservative jurists and progressive academics today describe as fundamentally new.[10]

Against this well-known picture of three successive regimes, the legacies of losing that we have described in chapters 2, 3, and 4 offer a more complex interpretation of the trajectory of American politics. First, the constitutional junctures are not symmetrical—the first is more important than the subsequent two. Notwithstanding the seriousness of all three constitutional crises, we have had only one regime, not three. The Reconstruction and New Deal conflicts were generated by the political logic of the Founding and are conducted within the capacious and tension-filled confines of its political architecture. That is one reason the antagonists in these subsequent contests invoke competing conceptions of founding authority.

Second, American politics does have a trajectory more or less consonant with the political logic described by both Federalists and Anti-Federalists. As we mentioned above, an increasingly complex national economy, an increasingly urban political culture, and the nationalization of politics—to take three large obvious examples—were initiated and anticipated by constitutional commitments. There is a constitutional direction to American politics—both in terms of increasingly complex material forms and in terms of aspirations to more fully realized ideals.

Third, although there is a direction to American political development, predicted by opponents on both sides of the founding debate, that political development has been contested, challenged, impeded, and sometimes subverted by heirs to the Anti-Federalists, including most notably Andrew Johnson and Barry Goldwater. Because these challenges to the political logic of the Constitution have been so successful, the core constitutional logic is misunderstood or thought by many to be illegitimate, and the aspiration to more fully realize constitutional ideals is often frustrated or hampered by a persistent anticonstitutional tradition, often manifest, and referred to by scholars, as an illiberal tradition. This alternative tradition gains its authority partly by representing itself as the authentic constitutional understanding. Because one can trace a dominant Federalist strand through the two subsequent "victors" in these contests, and an Anti-Federalist strand through the initial "losers," the constitutional moments after the Founding operate within and at the same time reconfigure and appropriate the discourse of the original founding debate.

Fourth, although the major losers over the course of American political history sustain and deploy the Anti-Federal outlook and the winners extend the Federalist point of view, these traditions are not coherent. Some progressives and New Dealers deploy the Anti-Federal appropriation on particular issues, and Johnson and Goldwater incorporate some Federalist ideas into their ideology.

Finally, given that the Constitution's political logic continues to develop as predicted, the Anti-Federal element of both the winners' and losers' ideologies can be understood as layered on top of the Constitution's logic. Taken to be legitimate interpretations of the Constitution while at odds with its constitutive features and animating principles, these complex ideologies and policies sustain a political tradition that frustrates, impedes, retards, and sometimes subverts the political logic of the Constitution without derailing its trajectory. This is the point that concluded chapter 1, and we hope that in light of our three cases it will be clearer now.

Liberal Consensus, Multiple Traditions, and Appropriation

Ackerman, Lowi, and Burnham argue that American politics has not been seamlessly progressive because it has been punctuated by disruptive change at the most fundamental level. At the same time, in their rendering, the course of American political development has been a linear movement in a liberal or progressive direction. Both aspects of their developmental account owe much to the influential ideas of Louis Hartz.[11]

Following Tocqueville, Hartz argued that because America did not require a social revolution to establish its democracy, because it lacked a feudal tradition to overcome, liberalism (understood as a commitment to equality and to rights) has dominated America's self-understanding and has accounted for the absence of viable socialist and fascist parties and movements over the course of American history. As Stephen Skowronek cogently states: "In *The Liberal Tradition*, Hartz acknowledged that American society was rife with material for fundamental conflict but found the political expression of antithetical ends stifled by the encompassing quality and unrivaled status of liberal precepts."[12]

Not only do scholars of transformative change see the overall trajectory of American politics as consistent with the Hartzian thesis but they also depict the periods between disruptive changes—periods of so-called normal politics—as marked by liberal ideological hegemony. In their accounts, transformative moments bring a victory so complete that the winner's new, more progressive definition of liberalism is one to which all are presumed to acquiesce either out of genuine conversion or simply to maintain political relevancy. Each "constitutional moment" revised fundamental features of the American political regime—the concepts and categories through which the polity understood the political world, the political practices learned and eventually taken for granted, the interests recognized as having rightful policy claims, the institutions inhabited, and the boundaries set for legitimate political debate. Thus, the politician's constant desire to win, to acquire or hold on to office, forges a new consensus around the newly dominant interpretation of liberalism.

Again, we argue that these well-known transformative successes were not as thorough or unequivocal as is conventionally assumed. In each of these new eras, the "losers" managed to maintain more than a foothold. This observation, which we previously discussed with respect to agency, also complicates the conventional narrative of liberal progress and consensus.[13]

Our account of America's contested constitutional moments amplifies and supplements recent revisions to the Hartz thesis. Rogers Smith showed that Hartz and his many followers ignored or dismissed the presence and significance of an antiliberal, ascriptive tradition in American politics. American politics was "liberal" but it was also, at the same time, fundamentally antiliberal or illiberal. Smith's work reveals three American traditions: liberal, republican, and ascriptive.[14] Others have endeavored to show that not only can liberalism and illiberalism coexist but that the two can also be imbricated in each other in complex ways. Stephen Skowronek has shown that the ideas of liberalism can be infused with antiliberal purposes and meanings.[15] Michael Rogin showed how liberalism itself fostered many illiberal ideas and practices—that a seemingly sunny liberalism had a dark side.[16] And while not drawing explicitly on the American experience, Uday Mehta has shown how the demands of liberalism have historically been interpreted so as to legitimate particular ascriptively assigned, or illiberal, exclusions.[17] Collectively, these authors demonstrate the vitality of antiliberal ideas and practices and reveal their complex relationship to liberalism.

Much of what has been described as America's liberal tradition can be summarized through reference to the victors at each of the three great constitutional moments. And much of what has been described as America's antiliberal tradition can be traced to the losers of these same contests. (Indeed, we believe that one of the reasons the Anti-Federalists, Andrew Johnson, and Barry Goldwater are so roundly and soundly dismissed in historical remembrance may have to do with the sense that they represent the polity's antiliberal instinct. Dismissing them as irrelevant allows the polity to move forward, confident in its liberal progress.) The mechanisms of agency that we discussed earlier in this chapter help to account for how these alternative traditions took hold and are sustained across time. In Rogers Smith's telling, evidence for the existence and significance of these alternative traditions is more vivid than is an account of the mechanisms that sustained them. As he writes, "When older types of ascriptive inequality, such as slavery, have been rejected as unduly illiberal, it has been normal, not anomalous, for many Americans to embrace new doctrines and institutions that reinvigorate the hierarchies they esteem in modified form."[18] The chapters on Andrew Johnson and Barry Goldwater show how these hierarchies have been reinvigorated for so many Americans. These traditions have been sustained, not by accident, but at least partly as a result of the purposeful intervention of key American "losers" and the effects of their actions.

These cases also have the advantage of isolating moments of constitutive significance—moments in which what is decided politically shapes the way Americans subsequently think. Cases of constitutional contestation allow us to see the terms and categories the political actors invented for themselves and for their posterity—terms and categories actually operative in the polity—rather than imposing our own scholarly categories, or those of others, on the political material. Our central political actors, the antagonists in the three constitutional contests, rarely described themselves as "liberal" and still more rarely, perhaps never, as "illiberal," "antiliberal," or "ascriptive." Of course, some who described themselves as liberal engaged in practices that we would rightly label antiliberal or illiberal. But our cases of losers show the opposite to also be true—that political actors some would describe as antiliberal or illiberal occasionally made powerful liberal arguments. These seeming paradoxes are even more vivid if one observes the constitutional categories and language actually used rather than the broader abstraction of liberalism. The sounder constitutional argument was sometimes made by the loser. Rather than two coherent and contending traditions, a truer picture of important political alternatives shows contending sides with dominant and subsidiary aspects.

This pattern that we have discovered lends support to Rogers Smith's "multiple traditions" thesis:

> At its heart, the multiple-traditions thesis holds that the definitive feature of American political culture has been not its liberal, republican, or "ascriptive Americanist" elements but, rather, this more complex pattern of apparently inconsistent combinations of the traditions, accompanied by recurring conflicts. Because standard accounts neglect this pattern, they do not explore how and why Americans have tried to uphold aspects of all three of these heterogeneous traditions, in combinations that are longer on political and psychological appeal that on intellectual coherency.[19]

Stephen Skowronek objects to the use of tradition as a category, warning that juxtaposing liberal and ascriptive traditions "risks reification and encumbers more direct assessments of how racists and liberal objectives impact one another." As the above quotation from Rogers Smith makes clear, Smith sees the "traditions" as less than coherent and also as overlapping, so we read Skowronek's account of the mutual relation of ideas and purposes as an improved rendering of Smith's multiple traditions thesis rather than a refutation of it. Because we do find a discernible, though less than fully coherent, line connecting the Federalists, Lincoln, and FDR, on the one hand, and the Anti-Federalists, Andrew Johnson, and Barry Goldwater, on the other, like Smith, we think it still fair to contend that there are ideological traditions in American political development. Each line of ideology and practice is not coherent and each borrows from, and inter-

sects with, the other, so Skowronek is right to warn against over-
stating or reifying these traditions. Yet these lines of influence are
distinctive and coherent enough to justify distinguishing them
from one and another. For that reason, we retain the language
of traditions though now as variants of a broad constitutional
discourse rather than disputes regarding the academic category
of liberalism and its alternatives.

That said, in our view Skowronek's critique reframes the multiple traditions idea in ways that are very helpful here. Our complex picture of the legacy of conflict at America's most significant
constitutional junctures supports and profits from his account.
Skowronek was prompted to develop a theory of the role of ideology by two seeming paradoxes. Progressive thinkers, such as
Arthur Schlesinger, multiculturalists, and contemporary legal
academics such as Lani Guinier, have rediscovered the theory
of concurrent majorities that John Calhoun invented to justify
the legitimacy of slavery in southern states. This loser's ideology, discredited for more than eighty years, has been revived and
deployed to advance purposes diametrically opposed to those for
which it was originally invented. President Woodrow Wilson,
arguably America's founding father of Progressivism, deepened
and extended—some have argued "radicalized"—American liberal commitments at the very same time that he defended racist practices, institutions, and ideas. Skowronek uses the case
of Woodrow Wilson to explain these seeming paradoxes and
thereby illustrate the way ideas actually work to shape the course
of American political development.

To make the study of ideology and change more systematic,
Skowronek distinguishes three moves by political actors: "the
appropriation of ideas within the tradition, the transposition of
ideas from one context to another, and the interaction of appropriated ideas with new purposes in the construction of meaning."
This formulation more precisely describes some of the ways in
which the winners and losers in our account appropriated and
redeployed Federalist and Anti-Federal ideas combining them in
unexpected ways and attaching them to new purposes.

In turn, our account adds two dynamics to the three that Skowronek identified. First, we identify an important form of appropriation that is unique to American political life. Heirs to the Anti-Federalists not only redeploy Federalist ideas for new purposes but they also exploit the iterative form in which the original ideas were expressed. Second, we suggest that ideas concerning the Constitution operate simultaneously on two levels. One level is the level Skowronek describes so well, the conscious appropriation and deployment of ideas for new purposes. In our rendering, this level reveals two complex traditions, each with a dominant and subsidiary aspect. We have tried to show how, over time, these four strands are braided for reasons Skowronek describes so well. The second level is the ideas that actually inform the operation of the Constitution and the development of the polity whether or not citizens and politicians are conscious of them. This second level is the "political logic" that we have discussed at some length in chapter 2 and that formed the deep, but ironic, source of complete agreement at the Founding. American political development can be characterized as the working out of ideas at each level and, simultaneously, the layering of the complex of braided ideas on top of the regime's political logic.

The ironic history of the Bill of Rights illustrates this complex ideational dynamic. The meaning of the Bill of Rights in constitutional interpretation and American political culture today is very different from that anticipated by Federalists and Anti-Federalists. Contrary to conventional wisdom, the addition of the Bill of Rights was not an Anti-Federal victory. However, over the long term, the features of the Bill of Right designed to advance the Federalist cause have been ignored or muted and in practice the Bill of Rights works more like one feared by the Federalists than the one they preferred and thought they had crafted. As with the Constitution as a whole, the Anti-Federalists lost the fight for a bill of rights but their alternative vision gained traction over the long run.

As we mentioned in chapter 2, the standard and well-known view is that extracting the promise of a bill of rights during ratification and amending the Constitution in the First Congress is one important way that the Anti-Federalists won in the immediate contest. That the Federalists gave us the Constitution but the Anti-Federalists gave us the Bill of Rights is the usual story. This is one instance where conventional wisdom has credited the loser with long-term success. We would not have a bill of rights but for the Anti-Federalist criticism of the Constitution for lacking one. Anti-Federal leaders at the Massachusetts ratifying convention were on the verge of defeating ratification when Federalists, led by the late intervention of John Hancock, promised that adding a bill of rights would be one of the first orders of business after the Constitution was ratified. Though the Federalists persuaded a majority of delegates not to make ratification contingent on a bill of rights, they persuasively and firmly promised one. That promise was taken up by subsequent ratifying conventions where it also made a difference in the outcome.

These well-known facts seem to support our thesis that the losers were actually winners in a very important respect while diminishing our claims to originality on this point. Yet both of these conclusions are wrong. The Anti-Federalists did lose initially and they did win, again, in the long run. However, these counterconventional claims do not evidence Anti-Federal appropriation, the subject of chapter 2. Here, the political dynamic developed in ways that ran contrary to the expectations of both sides. Rather than a direct result of a political strategy, the use of the Bill of Rights, and the protection of rights more generally, developed from an unanticipated braiding of Federal and Anti-Federal positions layered on top of the political logic of the Constitution.[20]

The Bill of Rights that was crafted by the First Congress of the United States was a defeat for the Anti-Federalists at the time. The effort was designed and led by James Madison to solidify the Federalist victory. Having won a decisive majority in the First Congress, most Federalists were willing to postpone the issue of amendments to the Constitution to attend to the immediately pressing business of standing up a brand new government, indeed a new administrative state, and some were willing to renege on the commitment altogether. Madison repeatedly urged his fellow congressmen to take up the issue. He argued that the commitment to the Anti-Federalists and indeed to the American people needed to be fulfilled because it was simply the right thing to do and because doing the right thing was also necessary to the legitimacy of the new regime. But his most important argument was partisan and strategic: he urged that the large majority offered Federalists an opportunity to get amendments that they preferred and that advanced their political project. Delaying or reneging would enable those of the Anti-Federal persuasion, elected in some future Congress, to craft amendments that would repeal the most essential features of the Constitution.

During the ratification debate, both sides agreed that protection of rights was a fundamental purpose of modern politics. In this respect, both sides were liberals. However, the Anti-Federalists perceived the main threat to individual rights to be a strong centralized government while the Federalists perceived rights to be less secure under state governments than in a new national regime. Because the Anti-Federalists thought the threat greatest from government, especially a distant and powerful government, they urged that sovereignty should primarily attach to smaller state governments that were relatively close and accountable to their citizenry. The Federalists understood the problem of rights to stem primarily from society, from pernicious factions, especially majority factions. They argued that states were already too large to provide the traditional advantages of small republics but not large enough to be sites for a new kind of political regime based on a new political science. In *Federalist* No. 10, Madison offers his now classic argument for a large extended republic as a new solution to the problem of factions and for the protection of rights.

Because Anti-Federalists modeled their understanding of the problem of rights on the state experience and existing state constitutions, they urged bills of rights as a way to educate the citizenry as well as to offer legal protection against the state. This meant that they favored constitutional forms that made rights far more prominent and central to the text than the Bill of Rights that was eventually adopted. More important, in the context of the proposed constitution, their main concern was the diminished power of the states, rather than rights per se. Their advocacy for individual rights during ratification was principally a vehicle to challenge matters of structure and power in the proposed constitution and new regime.

The Federalist chose to respond to the Anti-Federalist challenge regarding a bill of rights by defending the rights-protecting features of the Constitution. Hamilton argued that the Constitution itself was a bill of rights. By this he meant that there were particular rights explicitly protected in the body of the document, like the proscription of ex post facto laws, that other rights were implied in features of the Constitution such as the republican guarantee clause, and most important, that rights would best be protected by structurally induced conflict in the new kind of separation of powers that the Constitution contained. The actual operation of government, rather than the announcement of rights, was the key to rights protection, in *The Federalist*. Hamilton also argued that rights would be less secure with a bill of rights than without one. He stressed that the listing of rights explicitly would imply that citizens did not have specific rights that were not on that list. Instead of an exclusive focus on rights, per se, *The Federalist* vision pointed to the possibility of a jurisprudence of power—a potential civic and legal discourse about the appropriateness of power in instances of its exercise.

In the First Congress, Madison crafted a bill of rights that responded to stated Anti-Federal concerns about the security of individual liberties and to Hamilton's hesitations. His amendments listed rights the Anti-Federalists had demanded while also adding what became the Ninth and Tenth Amendments that underscored the principle that rights not included on the list were nevertheless preserved. He revealed the Anti-Federalists to be genuinely more interested in state power than in individual rights by proposing that the amendment protecting freedom of religion and proscribing religious establishment be explicitly extended to the states. Anti-Federalists resisted this and in doing so revealed that preserving state power was a higher priority for them than protecting individual rights.

One very interesting issue that emerged in the First Congress debate was the question of how to frame amendments to the Constitution? Should the Bill of Rights be added to the beginning of the Constitution as in several of the state constitutions? As a series of "whereas" statements preceding the Preamble, this prominence would signify the central importance of rights and also serve as a vehicle for civic education. Or should the amendments be integrated into the original document, literally amending some clauses and inserting others within the existing text? This placement might diminish the significance of the amendments by their diffusion and integration into the preexisting text. Or should the amendments come at the end, as footnotes or elaborations to the document left with its original structure intact? The Anti-Federalists preferred option one. Madison (then still a Federalist) preferred options two and three. The third option was chosen. Federalists hoped that this choice would diminish the significance of the amendments by underscoring what the document already implied rather than signifying any truly constitutive changes.

Thus, the adoption of the Bill of Rights was a Federalist victory. It articulated rights that Federalists thought the Constitution already recognized. It did not foreclose other natural or human rights that were not explicitly listed. The Bill of Rights was crafted in a way that preserved the Constitution's primary emphasis on structure and power and the operation of government as a way to best secure rights and advance the common good. Preempting later Anti-Federalist draftsmen, the Federalists thought they had diminished the significance of a bill of rights and enhanced the significance of the Constitution to which it was appended. Most important, Madison *prevented* the adoption of structural amendments that, were the Anti-Federalist to prevail, would have restored state power and authority and diminished the federal government. These were the Anti-Federalists' highest priority, as they had been during the drafting and ratification of the original Constitution. The Anti-Federalists were big losers once again.

Over the course of American history, however, Hamilton's worries have proven prescient and the practices of interpretation have advanced Anti-Federal objectives and have somewhat undermined the Federalist project. Contrary to Federalist expectations, the placement of the Bill of Rights at the tail end of the document did not diminish its significance but rather enhanced it. Indeed, most Americans know much more about the Bill of Rights than they do about the Constitution to which it is appended. One could say that in modern constitutional politics the tail wags the dog. It is also the case that notwithstanding the Ninth Amendment, Courts have tended to exhibit the pathology that worried Hamilton. If rights are not explicitly mentioned it is common for many jurists to insist that they do not exist in the Constitution. The right to privacy is a good example. That such a right can be inferred from other rights that are mentioned in the Constitution—or that it is a right that simply inheres in human beings by nature—are notions mocked by modern conservatives in the Anti-Federal tradition who insist that matters such as abortion be left to the discretion of state power.[21]

As Mary Ann Glendon has observed, American political discourse is essentially "rights talk."[22] We do not have a robust civic sphere where rights are an important theme within a larger discourse about the common good. Nor do we have a robust discussion of power and its limits as a means of securing rights. Our focus is on rights and legal vindication. Both the Federalists and the Anti-Federalists sought to protect and secure rights. But they differed profoundly on how best to do that. The centrality of the Bill of Rights in the contemporary constitutional order is, in the end, one of the most important and decisive Anti-Federalist victories, albeit in ways that they did not plan or anticipate.

Synoptic Synthesis

We conclude by stressing that the major synoptic accounts of American politics need to be conjoined and supplemented, not abandoned or replaced. American politics has been punctuated by moments of unusual transformation and massive change. Scholars of regime change are right to mark those episodes as critical and to explain and assess the transformative effects of the victors. In documenting the extraordinary long-term influence of the losers at each one of America's major constitutional moments, we mean to urge an account of American political development that takes note of the complex interaction of major "winners" and "losers" and the ways in which these interactions sustain multiple traditions within a single identifiable constitutional regime.

When Herbert Storing began research on his remarkable study of the Anti-Federalists, he reported that his interest in the topic was provoked by a quest for a coherent alternative to liberalism as a political foundation. Perhaps, he thought, the Anti-Federalists offered a modern version of a vision of politics understood as a form of political community over and above the individual citizens that composed it. On such a vision, politics would be about satisfying the needs and advancing the purposes of community more than it would be about protecting or advancing individual rights. He did not find what he anticipated. Like the Federalists, the Anti-Federalists were liberals—in the sense that politics was fundamentally about protecting and vindicating individual rights. To be sure, the Anti-Federalists did urge community, particularly at the local level, and they sharply criticized the Federalists' understanding of a diverse and pluralistic regime of continental scope as posing severe problems for viable communities and potentially leading to some form of tyranny. But Storing's point was that even the Anti-Federalists saw community as an instrumental good in the service of individual rights. They urged that rights were more secure in communities at the state and local level than in a massive and unprecedented experiment in democracy on a continental scale. Communities and their autonomous purposes were not ends in themselves. Individual rights remained the fundamental ends of politics and different versions of community were offered as contending means to secure rights. Thus, at bottom, both the Federalists and the Anti-Federalists were liberals. The truth of this insight is one reason that the Hartz thesis was never entirely refuted by subsequent critics. And it is a deep source for our own claims that America has had only one regime, not three, and that there has been a progressive direction to the regime notwithstanding many roadblocks and subversions.[23]

In the American political tradition, republicanism is subsumed within liberalism rather than a fundamental alternative to it.[24] Rogers Smith's bracketing of the republican tradition and his difficulty in finding a name for the counterliberal tradition—which he labels "ascriptive"—make sense in light of America's liberal origins. America's contending traditions stem from a shared political framework—liberalism as expressed in the Constitution. That is why illiberal practices and policies rarely announce themselves as such. We have no "ascriptive" party or aristocratic party in the United States. Instead, we have contending interpretations of the liberal framework. The ascriptive tradition in America gains some of its power from this very fact—that it too cites the Constitution or constitutional resources like *The Federalist* for its authority.

We have previously discussed the political logic of the Constitution described by Federalists and Anti-Federalists. The aspects we emphasized were the institutional, policy, and cultural implications that stem from core commitments embedded in the Constitution. The political logic also has an aspirational aspect stemming from core normative constitutional principles. The basic commitment to rights, shared by Federalists and Anti-Federalists, has expanded over time. One reason the ascriptive tradition went relatively unnoticed in political science until Rogers Smith called such attention to it is that political argument in the United States is expressed in rights terms derived from the Constitution or its interpretation. Rights are the vehicle and the terrain of contestation for contending partisans in America. Whether the rights of the unborn versus the rights of women, the rights of gun owners versus the rights of citizens to be safe from gun owners, or the locus of rights protection at the state versus the national levels, claims for exclusion as well as inclusion appropriate constitutional language and gain rhetorical legitimacy as a result.

The logic of these appropriations of constitutional text is remarkably similar to the structure of rhetoric in *The Federalist*. The Constitution included (and still includes) provisions designed to facilitate its launch that were inconsistent with its core principles. These provisions were intended to fall away or be overwhelmed by core commitments because of the political logic of the design. In chapter 2, we discussed the iterated cases for nationalism and the abandonment of separation of powers as traditionally understood. These rhetorical strategies are reflected in the language and structure of the Constitution itself. Thus, for example, there is little support for states qua states in the Constitution, but there is plenty of language about states that was designed to bring them on board and that is later invoked on their behalf, as our chapters on Andrew Johnson and Barry Goldwater demonstrate.

One can see this structure or pattern more vividly in the decisions regarding slavery that were necessary to secure ratification of the Constitution. The original Constitution contains three provisions offered as compromises to southern states: a clause prohibiting Congress from banning the importation of slaves until 1808; a clause requiring free states to return fugitive slaves to slave states; and a clause that states for purposes of representation and taxation slaves shall be counted as three-fifths of a free person. Do these compromises define the Constitution as a proslavery project, or are they better understood as necessary features of an antislavery Constitution?

The great thinker and abolitionist Frederick Douglass began his public career as an unequivocal opponent of the Constitution because of these three commitments to slavery. Because of them, Douglass regarded the Constitution as a "compact with the Devil." But Douglass changed his mind. Later in his career, Douglass articulated, indeed insisted upon, the opposite position—that the Constitution was a magnificent instrument of freedom—based on the very same clauses. The mature Douglass argued that none of these clauses were constitutive of the core aspirations of the Constitution, that all were designed as temporary measures necessary to establish a polity designed to advance principles of freedom. He likened these clauses to "scaffolding"—ugly temporary structures necessary to erect beautiful architecture, structures that conceal the beauty of the building while it is being built and are dismantled when construction is complete. This was also Lincoln's view, though we think Douglass expressed it even more articulately and authoritatively, as a former slave.[25]

Douglass's scaffolding resembles *The Federalist*'s early iterations of arguments regarding federalism and separation of powers both by being necessary to secure the new and just political construction and in being, unfortunately, available for appropriation by the canny and for misunderstanding by the naïve. On the one hand, the Constitution was adopted and over time the scaffolding came down as slavery was eliminated. It took a Civil War to do this; it was not a peaceful evolution as some had hoped it would be. Still, the Constitution generated both the conditions that led to war and the principles upon which the war would be fought. In those senses, the slavery clauses were inseparable from the forward-looking and somewhat progressive political logic of the Constitution. On the other hand, slavery was not merely a legally enforced status; it was also an aspect of a larger southern way of life with all sorts of attendant practices and attitudes bound to it. As we described in chapter 3, Andrew Johnson was willing to end the status of slavery, but he opposed Reconstruction efforts to contend with everything that surrounded the legal status—especially the economic and citizenship needs of newly freed slaves. We rehearse this familiar story to illustrate how all three aspects of our revision of the multiple traditions thesis are in play and intersect: an underlying political/constitutional logic and competing arguments layered over that developmental logic also fashioned with different political resources drawn from the same constitutional material.

Nonetheless, Douglass's belief and hope for the constitutional project has not been realized. The scaffolding was not fully dismantled because of the legacies of loss in American politics. One can see this poignantly today in the Black Lives Matter movement and the political rhetoric surrounding the shooting of police officers. It would be reasonable to read President Obama's nuanced rhetoric in the aftermath of the shootings as a practical effort to unify the country and avoid the sort of extensive violence that attended earlier episodes of racial strife. And surely, this was one of his principal objectives as he navigated, on the one hand, criticism from some for devoting his attention to the killing of police officers at a memorial service in Dallas yet not attending services for black citizens killed by police in Baton Rouge and Minneapolis while, on the other hand, receiving criticism for undermining law and order by sympathizing with the Black Lives Matter movement in his eulogy to police officers.

But if one looks carefully at President Obama's rhetoric, one can see that it is not just an attempt to be evenhanded and to encourage comity and unity—though it is that; it is also a picture of the complicated political development that we have attempted to describe here. When Obama, speaking at the memorial service for the slain Dallas police officers, said, "Race relations have improved dramatically in my lifetime. Those who deny it are dishonoring the struggles that helped us achieve that progress," he paid homage to a constitutionally induced trajectory of liberalism that Frederick Douglass described. Yet he went on to say, "But we know—but, America, we know that bias remains. We know it. Whether you are black or white or Hispanic or Asian or Native American or of Middle Eastern descent, we have all seen this bigotry in our own lives at some point. . . . Although most of us do our best to guard against it and teach our children better, none of us is entirely innocent. No institution is entirely immune. And that includes our police departments. We know this," and in this way he is calling attention to the continuation of the ascriptive tradition. But more than that, he is underscoring the difficulty of seeing the phenomena that he described because of the powerful hold of the narrative of liberal progress. He needed to repeat that "we know this" precisely because we do not recognize what we know. We have detailed the mechanisms by which these aspects of the legacies of losing in American politics have been sustained for centuries but have been largely unacknowledged.[26]

Frederick Douglass's scaffolding metaphor was constructed to explain and justify the features of the Constitution that perpetuated slavery for a time. It is a rich and compelling metaphor that continues to be a resource for explaining the difficult subject of race in contemporary America. The power of his idea—and the fact that it did not fully work in the ways that Douglass anticipated—can inform the broader array of topics that mark constitutional contestation at each of the three major junctures of American history. To secure victory at the Founding, the Federalists made a series of compromises—on slavery, but also on the status of states and on the articulation of power—that advanced a project of liberalism on a continental scale. All of these compromises were in service of building a new regime with core principles in tension with, or antithetical to, those that marked the compromises. As we described with respect to race, Douglass was too optimistic that the scaffolding would be completely deconstructed as the polity was built. Parts of the scaffolding remain and over time the ideas represented by the metaphor became so ingrained in American political culture that as a practical matter the remnants of the scaffold have become attributes of the building. Our three cases of loss in American politics show how this has happened.

American politics is a liberal polity, even though it has a strong and long history of what we have called an antiliberal, or anticonstitutional, tradition. But American politics is not *simply* a liberal polity alongside a persistent antiliberal tradition. Its liberal tradition has antiliberal aspects, and America's antiliberal tradition, expressed and sustained by the losers of America's constitutional moments, is not unequivocally hostile to aspirations for justice and liberty. The beginning of wisdom about the character of American politics as a whole is the recognition that its competing political traditions, layered over the political logic of the Constitution, are asymmetrical, multifaceted, and braided.

Acknowledgments

This book is a true coauthorship. Every sentence was either composed or revised by both of us together in conversation. For this reason, the project took us nearly nine years. The logistics for this kind of collaboration required marathon writing sessions in Williamstown, Austin, New York, New Orleans, Philadelphia, San Francisco, Nashua, New Hampshire, and Bath, Maine. In between were many hours on Facetime. For putting up with all of this, indeed for helping us make it work, our most heartfelt thanks go to our spouses, Jean Ehrenberg and Paige Bartels. And to our daughters and sons: Elizabeth and Hanna; Rafael and Luca.

Because it is a coauthorship, our debts to colleagues and institutions are even greater than usual, and we would like to acknowledge them all. While we are tremendously grateful for the help we have received over these many years, we regret that we did not have the foresight to record every specific instance in which we gleaned insight and support. We do remember many. Generous support was provided by Williams College, through the Oakley Center for the Humanities and Social Sciences as well as through the Ursula Prescott Fund and the Sentinels of the Republic Fund. A year's research leave was supported by a Dean's Fellowship from the University of Texas at Austin and a Laurance S. Rockefeller Visiting Fellowship at the University Center for Human Values at Princeton. The American Political Development conference sponsored by Yale University's Center for the Study of American Politics supported the first draft of chapter 3. Claremont McKenna College hosted a workshop on American political thought and development at which parts of chapters 2 and 5 were discussed. A later version of chapter 2 was presented at the Program on Constitutional Government at Harvard University. Iterations of various chapters were presented throughout the years at meetings of the American Political Science Association and as lectures at Baylor University, Carroll College, Mercer University, and Williams College.

Special thanks go to Stephen Skowronek and Sidney Milkis, whose urging that we write a paper on Andrew Johnson and political agency germinated the idea that grew into this book. Very helpful comments and criticisms on early drafts of the Johnson chapter were provided by Marc Landy, David Siemers, Mariah Zeisberg, Mark Graber, Bruce Ackerman, Richard Valelly, Richard Bensel, Jacob Hacker, Elisabeth Clemens, James Morone, Ira Katznelson, Victoria Hattam, Bryan Garsten, Stephen Skowronek, and Matthew Glassman. Drafts of the chapter on Barry Goldwater benefited from comments by Terri Bimes, Curt Nichols, Gary Schmitt, Daniel Galvin, John DiIulio, David Crockett, and Bruce Miroff. The chapter on the Anti-Federalists was made better by conversations with Harvey Mansfield, Sandy Levinson, Willy Forbath, Shep Melnick, Tom Pangle, David Nichols, George Thomas, James Ceaser, Rogers Smith, James Morone, Elvin Lim, Susan McWilliams, David Schaefer, and Michael Zuckert. Valuable research assistance was provided by Jacob Eisler, Joseph Samuels, Emily Hertz, and Christine Bird.

For suggestions on the project as a whole we are especially grateful to Gary Jacobsohn, Sotirios Barber, Will Harris, Nan Keohane, Stephen Macedo, José Luis Martí, Jeffrey Abramson, Michael Aronson, Russell Muirhead, Emily Zackin, Sidney Milkis, John DiIulio, Justin Crowe, Jesse Rhodes, and the readers for the University of Chicago Press.

Our editor, Chuck Myers, has been supportive of this project from the beginning and is a true model of professional excellence. We also thank Carol McGillivray, Holly Smith, and the rest of the team at the University of Chicago Press. For assistance in the final stages, we are most thankful to Ira Katznelson. It should go without saying but we will say it: our talented and generous friends and colleagues should get credit for helping us improve the book, but any errors that remain are our own.

Portions of chapters 2 and 3 were published in earlier versions. We thank the following for their permission to revise, elaborate, and incorporate these previous publications: "Andrew Johnson and the Politics of Failure," in *Formative Acts: American Politics in the Making*, ed. Stephen Skowronek and Matthew Glassman (Philadelphia: University of Pennsylvania Press, 2007), © 2007 University of Pennsylvania Press; "The Anti-Federal Appropriation," *American Political Thought* 3, no. 1 (Spring 2014), © 2014 by the Jack Miller Center.

Finally, we are greatly indebted to the scholars whose pathbreaking work inspired us to attempt the challenge of a synoptic account of American politics that combines the study of thought and practice: Herbert J. Storing and Walter Dean Burnham, to whom we have dedicated this book, and Bruce Ackerman, Theodore Lowi, Anne Norton, Karen Orren, Michael Rogin, Stephen Skowronek, and Rogers Smith.

Austin, Texas, and Williamstown, Massachusetts,
December 2016

Notes

CHAPTER ONE

1. John R. Vile, *Presidential Winners and Losers: Words of Victory and Concession* (Washington, DC: CQ Press, 2002). Given his campaign rhetoric, had Donald Trump lost the 2016 election, he might not have upheld this norm, and that would surely have been regarded as abnormal. Trump would have been the exception that proved the rule. Like Gore's, in 2000, Hillary Clinton's 2016 concession was gracious.

2. Bruce Ackerman, *We the People*, vol. 1, *Foundations* (Cambridge, MA: Belknap Press, 1993); *We the People*, vol. 2, *Transformations* (Cambridge, MA: Belknap Press, 2000); *We the People*, vol. 3, *The Civil Rights Revolution* (Cambridge, MA: Belknap Press, 2014); and Ackerman, "Storrs Lectures: Discovering the Constitution," *Faculty Scholarship Series* (1984), Paper 149 (http://digitalcommons.law.yale.edu/fss_papers/149); Theodore Lowi, *The Personal President: Power Invested, Promise Unfulfilled* (Ithaca, NY: Cornell University Press, 1986); and Lowi, *The End of Liberalism: The Second Republic of the United States* (New York: W. W. Norton, 1979; republished 2009). Citations refer to the 1979 edition. Walter Dean Burnham, "Constitutional Moments and Punctuated Equilibria: A Political Scientist Confronts Bruce Ackerman's *We the People*," *Yale Law Journal* 108, no. 8 (June 1999): 2237–88; and Burnham, *Critical Elections and the Mainsprings of American Politics* (New York: W. W. Norton, 1971).

3. Alexis de Tocqueville, *Democracy in America*, Harvey Mansfield

and Delba Winthrop, eds. (Chicago: University of Chicago Press, 2000); Louis Hartz, *The Liberal Tradition in America* (New York: Harcourt, Brace, and World, 1955).

4. Samuel Huntington, *American Politics: The Promise of Disharmony* (Cambridge, MA: Belknap Press, 1981).

5. Rogers M. Smith, "Beyond Tocqueville, Myrdal, and Hartz: The Multiple Traditions in America," *American Political Science Review* 87, no. 3 (September 1993): 549–66; and Smith, *Civic Ideals: Conflicting Visions of Citizenship in U.S. History* (New Haven, CT: Yale University Press, 1997).

6. For a review of this debate over liberalism and its place in American political development (as well as an overview of the transformational moments debate), see Karen Orren and Stephen Skowronek, *The Search for American Political Development* (New York: Cambridge University Press, 2004), esp. ch. 2.

7. For examples, see Jane J. Mansbridge, *Why We Lost the ERA* (Chicago: University of Chicago Press, 1986); Seymour Martin Lipset and Gary Marks, *It Didn't Happen Here: Why Socialism Failed in the United States* (New York: W. W. Norton, 2001); Gerald Berk, *Alternative Tracks: The Constitution of American Industrial Order, 1865–1917* (Baltimore: Johns Hopkins University Press, 1997); Bruce Miroff, *The Liberals' Moment: The McGovern Insurgency and the Identity Crisis of the Democratic Party* (Lawrence: University Press of Kansas, 2007); Gerald N. Magliocca, *The Tragedy of William Jennings Bryan: Constitutional Law and the Politics of Backlash* (New Haven, CT: Yale University Press, 2014).

8. Ira Katznelson, *When Affirmative Action Was White: An Untold History of Racial Inequality in Twentieth-Century America* (New York: W. W. Norton, 2006). See also Katznelson's *Fear Itself: The New Deal and the Origins of Our Times* (New York: Liveright, 2014).

9. Mary Frances Berry, "Ronald Reagan and the Leadership Conference on Civil Rights: Battles Won and Wars Lost," in *Winning While Losing: Civil Rights, the Conservative Movement, and the Presidency from Nixon to Obama*, ed. Kenneth Osgood and Derrick E. White (Gainesville: University Press of Florida, 2014), 82.

10. Stuart Chinn, *Recalibrating Reform: The Limits of Political Change* (New York: Cambridge University Press, 2014).

11. For an example of the first, see Fred Greenstein, *The Hidden-*

Hand Presidency: Eisenhower as Leader (Baltimore: Johns Hopkins University Press, 1994; originally published by Basic Books, 1982); for the second, see Scott Farris, *Almost President: The Men Who Lost the Race but Changed the Nation* (Guilford, CT: Lyons Press, 2013).

12. Quoted in Jill Zuckman. "No Voting, More Anger on the Budget," *Boston Globe*, March 2, 1995, 1, as cited in Deborah Stone, *Policy Paradox: The Art of Political Decision Making*, 3rd ed. (New York: W. W. Norton, 2011), 2.

13. Stone, *Policy Paradox*, 2.

14. James Ceaser, *Presidential Selection: Theory and Development* (Princeton, NJ: Princeton University Press, 1979). For a contrary view on the history of parties, see John Gerring's *Party Ideologies in America* (Cambridge, MA: Harvard University Press, 1998).

15. Periodically, elections of great consequence have generated ideologically significant choice for voters and the results have shaken up this normally moderated partisan order. But in the wake of these critical elections, the usual moderated competition has returned under the auspices of a reframed political order. The realignment genre offers a rich literature on this historical pattern. For a basic overview of the historical pattern of realignments and party conflict, see James L. Sundquist, *Dynamics of the Party System*, rev. ed. (Washington, DC: Brookings Institution Press, 1983).

16. American Political Science Association, Committee on Political Parties, *Toward a More Responsible Two-Party System* (New York: Rinehart, 1950).

17. For a response to the authors of the American Political Science Association report and the argument that nonideological parties are good for stable governance, see Edward Banfield, "In Defense of the American Party System," in *Political Parties, U.S.A.*, ed. Robert A. Goldwin (Chicago: Rand McNally, 1961).

18. It is worth noting that for many scholars who study parties, winning office is always the central and animating feature of party design, even in today's polarized climate. As described by John H. Aldrich, author of *Why Parties? A Second Look* (Chicago: University of Chicago Press: 2011), parties are endogenous institutions designed (and occasionally redesigned) by ambitious office seekers and holders to facilitate winning elections. In this view, eras of conflict are a by-product of how politicians utilize parties to secure office. Other recent work suggests

that, while winning office is still the paramount drive for politicians, to do so today they must cater to the demands of their interest group and activist bases, and this generates conflict. This "group-centered" interpretation of parties (as opposed to the "politician-centered" model) suggests that interest groups, and their causes, now shape parties more than politicians do and is less optimistic about parties' moderating potential. See Kathleen Bawn, Martin Cohen, David Karol, Seth Masket, Hans Noel, and John Zaller, "A Theory of Political Parties: Groups, Policy Demands and Nominations in American Politics," *Perspectives on Politics* 10, no. 3 (2012): 571–97.

19. Wendy Hunter, *The Transformation of the Workers' Party in Brazil, 1989–2009* (New York: Cambridge University Press, 2010).

20. Stephen Skowronek, *The Politics Presidents Make: Leadership from John Adams to Bill Clinton,* 2nd ed., rev. (Cambridge, MA: Belknap Press, 1998).

21. This last point is illustrated by the extraordinary election of Donald Trump as president of the United States. It remains to be seen whether Trump's electoral success will actually enhance the conservative movement and the Republican Party, or undermine it. A watchful people would also be concerned with the fate of the constitutional order.

22. The conference led to an edited volume on the relationship between agency and structure: Stephen Skowronek and Matthew Glassman, eds., *Formative Acts: American Politics in the Making* (Philadelphia: University of Pennsylvania Press, 2007).

CHAPTER TWO

1. Peggy Noonan, "Obama Has a Good Day," *Wall Street Journal,* June 29, 2012; National Federation of Independent Business v. Sebelius, 567 US 8 (2012) (Scalia, Kennedy, Thomas, and Alito, JJ, dissenting).

2. Sebelius, 567 US at 29 (Roberts, C.J.).

3. Publius [James Madison, Alexander Hamilton, and John Jay], *The Federalist Papers* [1788], ed. Clinton Rossiter (New York: Penguin Putnam, 2003). All subsequent references in the text to *The Federalist* are to the Rossiter edition, which is titled *The Federalist Papers,* according to a twentieth-century convention. The original collection of essays was titled *The Federalist: A Collection of Essays, Written in Favor of the New Constitution, as Agreed upon by the Federal Convention, September 17, 1787.* For most of American history, this text has been referred to as *The Fed-*

eralist. For this reason and for ease of expression, we will use *The Federalist.* We designate each reference by the number of the paper and the now-known author, but we agree with Herbert J. Storing's view that the pseudonym *Publius* indicates an intention to present the argument as if authored by one voice, and that within *The Federalist,* there are no important differences between the positions expressed by Madison and those by Hamilton. For a classic statement of the contrary view, see Alpheus Thomas Mason, "The Federalist, A Split Personality," *American Historical Review* 57, no. 3 (April 1952): 625–43.

4. The main examples of Federalist audaciousness we review here are well known. For newly discovered details regarding the sources and extent of the Federalist victory, see the recent magisterial book on the entire founding period by Michael J. Klarman, *The Framers' Coup: The Making of the United States Constitution* (New York: Oxford University Press, 2016).

5. For discussions of the seeming paradox of unconstitutional constitutional amendments, see Gary Jeffrey Jacobsohn, *Constitutional Identity* (Cambridge, MA: Harvard University Press, 2010), and Walter F. Murphy, "An Ordering of Constitutional Values," *Southern California Law Review* 53 (1980): 703–60.

6. See Herbert Storing, ed., *The Complete Anti-Federalist,* vol. 1, *What the Anti-Federalists Were For* (Chicago: University of Chicago Press, 1981), 46.

7. See especially *Federalist* No. 10 (James Madison). Also, Martin Diamond, *As Far as Republican Principles Will Admit: Essays by Martin Diamond* (Washington, DC: AEI Press, 1991).

8. See Sheldon S. Wolin, *Presence of the Past: Essays on the State and the Constitution* (Baltimore, MD: Johns Hopkins University Press, 1990).

9. In his foreword to *Ratifying the Constitution,* Forrest McDonald insightfully points out, "When Congress and every state did as requested, they in effect amended the amending procedure prescribed by the Articles and thereby legitimated the whole enterprise." Forrest McDonald, foreword to *Ratifying the Constitution,* ed. Michael Allen Gillespie and Michael Lienesch (Lawrence: University Press of Kansas, 1989), ix.

10. McDonald, "Foreword," *Ratifying the Constitution,* ix.

11. Surveying the range of positions as they developed over the course of the ratification campaign, Klarman notes that "opinion on the

Constitution should be seen as existing along a continuous spectrum rather than being neatly divided into two camps." Klarman, *The Framers' Coup*, 310. While it is true that some Anti-Federalists, for example, would have been comfortable with a few small prescribed amendments to the Constitution and some Federalists, for example, were not harshly critical of the Articles as were most, the vote to ratify was an up or down vote. In that sense, as in all electoral contests where there is almost always a range of opinions on the matter contested, there were two sides in this contest.

12. Gillespie and Lienesch, *Ratifying the Constitution*, 5–17. See also Pauline Maier, *Ratification: The People Debate the Constitution 1787–1788* (New York: Simon and Schuster, 2011).

13. Madison forced the Anti-Federalists to reveal their true preferences when an amendment protecting freedom of religion and proscribing religious establishment was proposed. Madison urged that the amendment explicitly extend beyond the national government to include protection of religious freedom in the states. Herbert J. Storing, "The Constitution and the Bill of Rights," in *Toward a More Perfect Union*, ed. Joseph M. Bessette (Washington, DC: AEI Press, 1995), 112–13.

14. Storing, "The Constitution and the Bill of Rights," 111. As Storing further explains, "The whole emphasis on reservations of rights of individuals implied a fundamental acceptance of the 'consolidated' character of the new government. A truly federal government needs no Bill of Rights." Storing, *The Complete Anti-Federalist*, 1:65. For further details on the politics of the First Congress, see Klarman, "The Bill of Rights," chap. 7 in *The Framers' Coup*.

15. Maier, *Ratification*.

16. John Kaminski, Gaspare Saladino, Richard Leffler, Charles Schoenleber, and Margaret Hogan, eds., *The Documentary History of the Ratification of the Constitution* (Charlottesville: University of Virginia Press, 2016), is also available at http://rotunda.upress.virginia.edu/founders/RNCN.html. Historians writing on the period of ratification, including Maier, have benefited from this extraordinary compilation of documents, which is unprecedented in scope and depth and which will continue to be a treasure trove for historians for years to come. For those interested in classic historical accounts of the founding period more generally, see Gordon Wood, *The Creation of the American Repub-*

lic, 1776–1787 (Chapel Hill: University of North Carolina Press, 1969; reprinted with preface in 1998); Andrew Cunningham McLaughlin, *The Confederation and the Constitution: 1783–1789* (New York: Harper, 1905); Merrill Jensen, *The Founding of a Nation: A History of the American Revolution, 1763–1776* (New York: Oxford University Press, 1968; reprinted Hackett, 2004); and, as previously mentioned, Klarman, *The Framers' Coup*, which has a very useful bibliography.

17. This strategic rhetorical move was blasted by "Anti-Federalists." The Federal Farmer went so far as to differentiate "honest" from "pretended" Federalists: "Some of the advocates [of the Constitution] are only pretended federalists; in fact they wish for an abolition of the state governments. Some of them I believe to be honest federalists, who wish to preserve *substantially* the state governments united under an efficient federal head; and many of them are blind tools without any object." In this letter (VI, December 25, 1787), the Federal Farmer also recognized the Federalist willingness to support amendments as the political ploy that it was and warned citizens that "some of them [advocates of the Constitution] will only consent to recommend indefinite, specious, but unimportant ones; and this only with a view to keep the door open for obtaining, in some favourable moment, their main object, a complete consolidation of the states, and a government much higher toned, less republican and free than the one proposed." See "Federal Farmer VI," reprinted in Herbert Storing, ed., *The Complete Anti-Federalist.* All subsequent references to Anti-Federalist writings are from Storing.

18. To see this practice in action, complete with a "re-" appropriation of the Federalist label, either intentional or inadvertent, one need look no further than The Federalist Society, the contemporary law and public policy organization dedicated to promoting conservative views that are most consistent, at least on the issue of federalism, with Anti-Federal ideas.

19. David J. Siemers, *Ratifying the Republic: Antifederalists and Federalists in Constitutional Time* (Stanford, CA: Stanford University Press, 2002), xi; Jack N. Rakove, "Early Uses of *The Federalist*," in *Saving the Revolution: The Federalist Papers and the American Founding*, ed. Charles R. Kesler (New York: Free Press, 1987), 239. Klarman suggests that a booming economy and Madison's securing a bill of rights help explain how the new Constitution gained legitimacy so quickly. He also points out that "of critical significance, former Anti-federalists quickly

discovered that working within the new system would be at least as effective as attacking its legitimacy." Klarman stresses the unresolved issues of the Constitution as the avenue for Anti-Federal engagement. Here we show how the Anti-Federalists were able to exploit Federalist rhetoric *to reopen and reinterpret* issues that had been resolved by the adoption of the Constitution. Klarman, *The Framers' Coup*, 620.

20. Storing, *The Complete Anti-Federalist*, 1:6.

21. Modern-day unknowing Anti-Federalists, like Antonin Scalia, routinely turn to *The Federalist* as evidence of common eighteenth-century meanings of words and phrases used in the Constitution. See Antonin Scalia (Associate Justice, United States Supreme Court), interview with Piers Morgan, July 18, 2012, http://transcripts.cnn.com/TRANSCRIPTS/1207/18/pmt.01.html. Yet *The Federalist* does not share Scalia's orientation to "original meaning." Indeed *The Federalist* is as inventive of expression as it is reflective of common understandings of the time. See also H. Jefferson Powell, "The Original Understanding of Original Intent," *Harvard Law Review* 98 (1985): 885–948. As Sotirios Barber has shown, one common understanding that *The Federalist* does share with ordinary citizens is a commitment to moral realism, the view that abstract terms, like justice, refer to real ideals that can be approximated through improved understandings and can't be limited to the extant conventions or practices. This common-sense idea points to discovery of meaning over time rather than fixity in conventions of the time in which the Constitution was composed. This moral realist view of the world is shared by Anti-Federalists of the eighteenth century as well, though not by some of their twenty-first-century heirs like Scalia. See Sotirios Barber, *On What the Constitution Means* (Baltimore, MD: Johns Hopkins University Press, 1986); Sotirios Barber, "The Ninth Amendment: Inkblot or Another Hard Nut to Crack?" *Chicago-Kent Law Review* 64, no. 67 (1988); and Sotirios Barber, "Whither Moral Realism in Constitutional Theory? A Reply to Professor McConnell," *Chicago-Kent Law Review* 64, no. 67 (1988): 111.

22. Another fine example of an analytically political rather than primarily historical approach, and also a useful contrast of interpretation of the Constitution to important historians such as Gordon Wood and Michael Klarman, is Clement Fatovic, *America's Founding and the Struggle over Economic Inequality* (Lawrence: University Press of Kansas, 2015).

23. Storing, *The Complete Anti-Federalist*, 1:6.

24. In an especially colorful essay on the proposed national government's power to tax, Brutus raises the possibility that "this power, exercised without limitation, will introduce itself into every corner of the city, and country" affecting every citizen in every act of daily life. And he worries that eventually "such a power must necessarily, from its very nature, swallow up all the power of the state governments." See Brutus VI, December 27, 1987.

25. Storing, *The Complete Anti-Federalist*, 1:9.

26. George Washington, "Letter to the President of Congress, Arthur St. Clair," in *The Records of the Federal Convention of 1787*, vol. 2, ed. Max Farrand (New Haven, CT: Yale University Press, 1911).

27. For example, with regard to the issue of taxation, Brutus warns that the national government could easily regulate the state governments' capacity to tax and thus, by controlling states' capacities to generate revenue, render the states entirely "dependent on the will of the general government for their existence." Brutus VI, December 27, 1787.

28. Alexis de Tocqueville, *Democracy in America*, ed. Harvey Mansfield and Delba Winthrop (Chicago: University of Chicago Press, 2000).

29. Brutus I, October 18, 1787.

30. Storing, *The Complete Anti-Federalist*, 1:35.

31. *Federalist* No. 39 (James Madison).

32. *Federalist* No. 17 (Alexander Hamilton).

33. *Federalist* No. 17 (Alexander Hamilton).

34. *Federalist* No. 27 (Alexander Hamilton). See also Madison's agreement with this Hamiltonian point in *Federalist* No. 46.

35. *Federalist* No. 23 (Alexander Hamilton).

36. *Federalist* No. 31 (Alexander Hamilton).

37. Quote is taken from Jeff Powell, "The Compleat Jeffersonian: Justice Rehnquist and Federalism," *Yale Law Journal* 91, no. 7 (June 1982): 1364. Full text of the letter is available in the *South Carolina Historical and Genealogical Magazine* 1, no. 1 (January 1900) and archived through JSTOR at http://archive.org/stream/jstor-27574891/27574891_djvu.txt.

38. "Descending from theory to practice there is no better book than *The Federalist*," said Jefferson. *Letter from Thomas Jefferson to Thomas Mann Randolph, Jr.*, May 30, 1790. National Archives, http://founders.archives.gov/documents/Jefferson/01-16-02-0264.

39. 1 *Annals of Cong.* 380 (1789). See also Bernard Manin, "Checks, Balances and Boundaries: The Separation of Powers in the Constitutional Debate of 1787," in *The Invention of the Modern Republic*, ed. Biancamaria Fontana (New York: Cambridge University Press, 1994).

40. Manin, *The Invention of the Modern Republic*, 41 (quoting Denatus and Cato in Storing).

41. *Federalist* No. 48 (James Madison).

42. *Federalist* No. 37 (James Madison).

43. *Federalist* No. 41 (James Madison). One would hardly know today that *both* the Anti-Federalists and the Federalists anticipated a future polity with a standing army. It is widely assumed that the Constitution reflected the general distrust of standing armies, but the political logic of the Constitution was absolutely clear to thoughtful observers in the eighteenth century. Nevertheless, the Anti-Federalist objection and initial Federalist mollification frame modern-day understandings of the so-called original constitution even among scholars today. See, for example, Stephen M. Griffin, "Bringing the State into Constitutional Theory: Public Authority and the Constitution," *Law & Social Inquiry* 16, no. 4 (Autumn 1991), and Rebecca U. Thorpe, *The American Warfare State: The Domestic Politics of Military Spending* (Chicago: University of Chicago Press, 2014).

44. Anti-Federalists were explicit in their concern that the president would possess the powers of a monarch and would be able to use them for ill purposes. An Old Whig (V, November 1, 1787) wrote that the new executive would "be a King as much a King as the King of Great Britain, and a King too of the worst kind;—an elective King." Cato (IV, November 8, 1787) worried that "if the president is possessed of ambition, he has power and time sufficient to ruin his country."

45. Brutus warned his countrymen, "The supreme court under this constitution would be exalted above all other power in the government, and subject to no control. . . . I question whether the world ever saw, in any period of it, a court of justice invested with such immense powers, and yet placed in a situation so little responsible." Brutus XV, March 20, 1788.

46. See Woodrow Wilson, *The New Freedom: A Call for the Emancipation of the Generous Energies of a People* (New York: Doubleday, 1913), http://www.gutenberg.org/files/14811/14811-h/14811-h.htm.

47. See Jeffrey K. Tulis, *The Rhetorical Presidency,* 2nd ed., rev.

(Princeton, NJ: Princeton University Press, 2017), for a detailed discussion of Woodrow Wilson's misunderstandings of *The Federalist*.

48. There were, of course, key advisers to FDR who understood the sophisticated Federalist argument on behalf of national power and defended the New Deal on those terms. And there were conservatives who understood and agreed with the Federalists' constitutional logic for expanding national power but denied that some of the problems FDR considered to be national problems were genuine national problems.

49. Senator Thomas Gore (D, OK), May 16, 1935, "Social Security Act: Hearings before the Committee on Finance, United States Senate, Seventy-Fourth Congress, First Session on H.R. 7260, An Act to Provide for the General Welfare by Establishing a System of Federal Old-Age Benefits, and by Enabling the Several States to Make More Adequate Provision for Aged Persons, Dependent and Crippled Children, Maternal and Child Welfare, Public Health, and the Administration of their Unemployment Compensation Laws; To Establish a Social Security Board; To Raise Revenue and for Other Purposes," May 7, 8, 9, 13–17, 1935, 176. Available at http://www.finance.senate.gov/imo/media/doc/74HrgSSAct.pdf.

50. H. Jefferson Powell, "The Compleat Jeffersonian: Justice Rehnquist and Federalism," *Yale Law Journal* 91, no. 7 (June 1982): 1369–70 (emphasis original).

51. Ronald Reagan, Remarks at the Bicentennial Observance of the Battle of Yorktown in Virginia, October 19, 1981, American Presidency Project, http://www.presidency.ucsb.edu/ws/index.php?pid=43151&st=founders&st1=founding+fathers.

52. Ronald Reagan, Remarks at the Annual Meeting of the National Governors' Association in Cincinnati, Ohio, August 8, 1988, American Presidency Project, http://www.presidency.ucsb.edu/ws/index.php?pid=36218&st=founders&st1=founding+fathers.

53. "Paul Ryan State of the Union Response: Speech addresses Spending, Healthcare, and More," January 25, 2011, available at http://www.huffingtonpost.com/2011/01/25/paul-ryan-state-of-the-un_n_813985.html.

54. Newt Gingrich, *A Nation Like No Other: Why American Exceptionalism Matters* (Washington, DC: Regnery, 2011), 12–13.

55. Gingrich, *A Nation Like No Other*, 112.

56. Sarah Palin, speech at "Restoring America" Tea Party of America

Rally in Indianola, Iowa, September 3, 2011, retrieved at SarahPAC, http://sarahpac.com/posts/governor-palins-speech-at-the-restoring -america-tea-party-of-america-rally-in-indianola-iowa-video-and -transcript.

57. Ron Paul, *Liberty Defined: 50 Essential Issues that Affect Our Freedom* (New York: Grand Central, 2011), 124.

58. Theda Skocpol and Vanessa Williamson, *The Tea Party and the Remaking of Republican Conservatism* (New York: Oxford University Press, 2013), 50.

59. See Sotirios A. Barber, *The Fallacies of States' Rights* (Cambridge, MA: Harvard University Press, 2013).

CHAPTER THREE

1. Our focus in this chapter is on the ideas and policy practices of Reconstruction, but it is worth noting that Andrew Johnson's leadership style and his defense against impeachment also reveal the pattern of immediate political failure followed by lasting influence. Johnson invented the political practice of "going public" and was rightly ridiculed as a demagogue. Indeed, one of the articles of impeachment was for his demagogic rhetoric. That charge was dropped when Johnson successfully framed the impeachment process as a legal rather than political matter. One hundred fifty years later, "going public" is a prescribed norm, not a deviant exercise, and the legalistic understanding of impeachment has also prevailed over the political interpretation. On going public, see Jeffrey K. Tulis, *The Rhetorical Presidency,* 2nd ed., rev. (Princeton, NJ: Princeton University Press, 2017); Theodore Lowi, *The Personal Presidency: Power Invested, Promise Unfulfilled* (Ithaca, NY: Cornell University Press, 1986); Samuel Kernell, *Going Public: New Strategies of Presidential Leadership,* 4th ed. (Washington, DC: CQ Press, 2006); on impeachment, see Jeffrey Tulis, "Impeachment in the Constitutional Order," in *The Constitutional Presidency,* ed. Joseph M. Bessette and Jeffrey K. Tulis (Baltimore, MD: Johns Hopkins University Press, 2009).

2. Edward A. Pollard, *The Lost Cause* (New York: E. B. Treat, 1866), 745.

3. See John Milton Cooper, *Breaking the Heart of the World: Woodrow Wilson and the Fight for the League of Nations* (Cambridge: Cambridge University Press, 2001); Tulis, *The Rhetorical Presidency,* 147–61.

4. As Pollard describes it, "the new President was sprung from a low order of life, and was what Southern gentlemen called a 'scrub.' In

qualities of mind it was generally considered that he had the shallowness and fluency of the demagogue; but in this there was a mistake." Pollard, *Lost Cause*, 744.

5. Albert Castel, *The Presidency of Andrew Johnson* (Lawrence: University Press of Kansas, 1979), 18–23; Eric L. McKitrick, *Andrew Johnson and Reconstruction* (Chicago: University of Chicago Press, 1960), 105.

6. Castel, *Presidency of Andrew Johnson*, 20.

7. Editorial, "The President's Usurpations," *Harper's Weekly*, April 11, 1868, http://app.harpweek.com/.

8. Johnson preferred the term "restoration" to "reconstruction" because it implied a return to the status quo ante, which was more or less how he envisioned the postwar settlement. On the use of the terms, see Glenna R. Schroeder-Lein and Richard Zuczek, *Andrew Johnson: A Biographical Companion* (Santa Barbara, CA: ABC-CLIO, 2001), 239.

9. Heather Cox Richardson, *The Death of Reconstruction: Race, Labor, and Politics in the Post-Civil War North, 1865–1901* (Cambridge, MA: Harvard University Press, 2004), 16.

10. Cotton production, for example, fell from 5 million bales in 1860 to just 300,000 bales in 1865. Castel, *Presidency of Andrew Johnson*, 14.

11. In 1865, northern Democrats held a quarter of the seats in Congress.

12. Editorial, "The President's Usurpations," 226.

13. It should be reiterated, explicitly, that many in the North were always skeptical of Johnson's allegiance to the cause of the Union, seeing in his actions instead consistent dedication to his home region. As it was put in *Harper's Weekly* in the aftermath of his impeachment trial, "That Andrew Johnson has betrayed the party that elected him, that he has lamentably perplexed and delayed reconstruction, that he is virtually in alliance with those who hope to defeat the legitimate consequences of the war, and is, therefore, an enemy of peace and the Union, we have never doubted, and have always steadily maintained." Editorial, "The Oath and the Evidence," *Harper's Weekly*, May 30, 1868, 338.

14. From Andrew Johnson's "Washington's Birthday Address," February 22, 1866. *The Papers of Andrew Johnson*, vol. 10, *February–July 1866*, ed. Paul H. Bergeron (Knoxville: University of Tennessee Press, 1992).

15. In general, however, Anti-Federalists had a more vibrant and conscience-based concern for slavery while Federalists had a more realist-based concern for the institution. The issue of slavery was primarily regionally divisive, uniting southern Federalists and Anti-

Federalists against northern Federalists and Anti-Federalists. See Michael J. Klarman, *The Framers' Coup: The Making of the United States Constitution* (New York: Oxford University Press, 2016), ch. 4.

16. Charles Ernest Chadsey, *The Struggle between President Johnson and Congress over Reconstruction* (New York: Columbia University Press, 1896), 65.

17. As quoted in Richard Franklin Bensel, *Yankee Leviathan: The Origins of Central State Authority in America, 1859–1877* (New York: Cambridge University Press, 1990), 357.

18. Castel, *Presidency of Andrew Johnson*, 50–51.

19. Chadsey, *Struggle between President Johnson and Congress*, 44–45; Michael Les Benedict, *The Fruits of Victory: Alternatives in Restoring the Union, 1865–1877* (Philadelphia: Lippincott, 1975), part 2, document 4.

20. Cox Richardson, *Death of Reconstruction*, 17.

21. Cox Richardson, *Death of Reconstruction*, 17–20.

22. Pollard, *Lost Cause*, 750.

23. See Rogers M. Smith, *Civic Ideals: Conflicting Visions of Citizenship in U.S. History* (New Haven, CT: Yale University Press, 1997), ch. 10.

24. As moderates moved toward the agenda of leading Radicals, they embraced proposals of black suffrage and civil rights and asserted the need for military oversight to ensure this, but they never fully embraced the Radical idea of confiscating and redistributing rebel land to former slaves. See Eric Foner, *Politics and Ideology in the Age of the Civil War* (New York: Oxford University Press, 1980), 130–37.

25. Martin E. Mantell, *Johnson, Grant, and the Politics of Reconstruction* (New York: Columbia University Press, 1973), 22; Castel, *Presidency of Andrew Johnson*, 103–5; McKitrick, *Andrew Johnson and Reconstruction*, 467–71.

26. Mantell, *Johnson, Grant, and the Politics of Reconstruction*, ch. 2.

27. Quoted in Eric Foner, *A Short History of Reconstruction. 1863–1877* (New York: Harper and Row, 1990), 136.

28. Mantell, *Johnson, Grant, and the Politics of Reconstruction*, ch. 4 and p. 98.

29. See Richard M. Valelly, *The Two Reconstructions: The Struggle for Black Enfranchisement* (Chicago: University of Chicago Press, 2004); Richard Franklin Bensel, *Yankee Leviathan: The Origins of Central State Authority in America, 1859–1877* (New York: Cambridge University Press, 1990), 348–63.

30. Mantell, *Johnson, Grant, and the Politics of Reconstruction*, 75–77.

31. Mantell, *Johnson, Grant, and the Politics of Reconstruction*, 134–36.

32. Johnson's tolerance, and even perhaps encouragement, of violence to suppress black political organization was not new. The most notorious incident occurred in the summer of 1866 when Unionists in Louisiana, dissatisfied with the largely former Confederate government, organized a convention in New Orleans. Local authorities tried to prevent the assembly and asked if Johnson would interfere with their actions. Not only did the president indicate that he would not interfere but he gave them permission to request military aid in support of their actions. While troops ultimately were not deployed to break up the convention, the encouragement from Johnson was seen by many at the time as facilitating the violent riot that ensued, in which local white citizens and police killed and injured scores of primarily black convention attendees. Not only did Johnson fail to condemn the action but he also blamed the riot on the actions of Radical members of Congress. It was the New Orleans riot that turned many Northerners against Johnson's Union Party in 1866 and convinced Congress of the need to increase their reconstructive efforts. For a more detailed chronology of events, see Schroeder-Lein and Zuczek, *Andrew Johnson*, 209.

33. Foner, *Politics and Ideology*, 122–25.

34. For examples, see Keith M. Finley, *Delaying the Dream: Southern Senators and the Fight against Civil Rights, 1938–1965* (Baton Rouge: Louisiana State University Press, 2008); Joseph Crespino, *In Search of Another Country: Mississippi and the Conservative Counterrevolution* (Princeton, NJ: Princeton University Press, 2007).

35. For more detail on each of these examples, see Finley, *Delaying the Dream*, 36, 49–53, 65, 84–92, and 203–7. Quote is from p. 65.

36. Crespino, *In Search of Another Country*, 11.

37. Crespino, *In Search of Another Country*, 19.

38. Crespino, *In Search of Another Country*. The phrase "practical segregation" was coined by James P. Coleman, governor of Mississippi from 1956 to 1960 (19).

39. Castel, *Presidency of Andrew Johnson*, 20.

40. Castel, *Presidency of Andrew Johnson*, 42–43.

41. Mantell, *Johnson, Grant, and the Politics of Reconstruction*, 18–20; Castel, *Presidency of Andrew Johnson*, 78–79.

42. Benedict, *Fruits of Victory*, 61.

43. For other economic and political considerations in the election

outcome, see C. Vann Woodward, *Reunion and Reaction: The Compromise of 1877 and the End of Reconstruction* (Boston: Little, Brown, 1951); Keith Ian Polakoff, *The Politics of Inertia: The Election of 1876 and the End of Reconstruction* (Baton Rouge: Louisiana State University Press, 1973). For a thoughtful discussion of the challenges of Republican coalition building during Reconstruction, see Valelly, *The Two Reconstructions.*

44. Joel Williamson, *The Crucible of Race: Black-White Relations in the American South since Emancipation* (New York: Oxford University Press, 1984), 132–35 and ch. 7.

45. The irony here is that Johnson was executing a leadership on behalf of the white South in ways akin to how scholars have described slaves resisting white oppression in the antebellum South. In his classic book, *Weapons of the Weak*, James Scott writes, "The history of resistance to slavery in the antebellum U.S. South is largely a history of foot dragging, false compliance, flight, feigned ignorance, sabotage, theft, and, not least, cultural resistance. These practices, which rarely, if ever, called into question the system of slavery, *as such*, nevertheless achieved far more in their unannounced, limited, and truculent way than the few heroic and brief armed uprisings about which so much has been written. The slaves themselves appear to have realized that in most circumstances their resistance could succeed only to the extent that it hid behind the mask of public compliance." While all of Johnson's obstructionist practices could be interestingly compared to slaves' efforts at resistance, here we note that his effort to legitimize his actions by shrouding it in constitutionality effectively hid it "behind the mask of public compliance." See James C. Scott, *Weapons of the Weak: Everyday Forms of Peasant Resistance* (New Haven, CT: Yale University Press, 1987), 34.

46. Matthew D. Lassiter, *The Silent Majority: Suburban Politics in the Sunbelt South* (Princeton, NJ: Princeton University Press, 2007); Kevin M. Kruse, *White Flight: Atlanta and the Making of Modern Conservatism* (Princeton, NJ: Princeton University Press, 2007).

47. While some of Johnson's actions and rhetoric regarding constitutional propriety was strategic, the president appears genuinely dedicated to the idea that he was a defender of Union and Constitution. In fact, he left instructions (which were followed) for after his death: "When I die, wrap my body in the flag of my country, pillow my head on its Constitution and carry it to one of those beautiful hills in Greene County and there let me sleep until resurrection morning." In Bob Cox, "Former President Andrew Johnson Eulogized in Greeneville in

1909," *Johnson City Press,* October 14, 2013, http://www.johnsoncitypress
.com/article/111710/former-president-andrew-johnson-eulogized-in
-greeneville-in-1909#ixzz3UljBpHgz.

48. Johnson, "Washington's Birthday Address."

49. Johnson, "Washington's Birthday Address."

50. Castel, *Presidency of Andrew Johnson,* 56–57; Mantell, *Johnson, Grant, and the Politics of Reconstruction,* 20.

51. Pollard, *The Lost Cause,* 748.

52. Pollard, *The Lost Cause,* 750.

53. Benjamin Hill, 1876 speech upon receiving the national flag from citizens of Ohio, in *Senator Benjamin H. Hill of Georgia: His Life, Speeches and Writing,* ed. Benjamin Hill Jr. (Atlanta, GA: H. C. Hudgins, 1891), 470; Stephen Skowronek, "The Reassociation of Ideas and Purposes: Racism, Liberalism, and the American Political Tradition," *American Political Science Review* 100, no. 3 (August 2006): 390. Also Rogin Kersh, *Dreams of a More Perfect Union* (Ithaca, NY: Cornell University Press, 2001).

54. The John Ford cavalry trilogy includes the John Wayne films *Fort Apache* (1948), *She Wore a Yellow Ribbon* (1949), and *Rio Grande* (1950).

55. See Richard B. Russell (D, GA), July 2, 1957, 85th Cong., 1st sess., remarks regarding Civil Rights Act of 1957, 10771-72, http://congressional.proquest.com/congressional/docview/t19.d20.cr-1957-0702?accountid=15054. According to Russell biographer Gerald Fite, the speech was critical in persuading sufficient members of Congress as well as President Eisenhower to pass a much weaker version of the legislation than that which was initially proposed. See Gilbert C. Fite, *Richard B. Russell, Jr., Senator from Georgia* (Chapel Hill: University of North Carolina Press: 1991), 336–43.

56. See Finley, *Delaying the Dream,* quotes on pp. 9–10.

57. In an anecdote about the denial of black office-holding rights that is recounted by Richard Valelly in his masterful book, *The Two Reconstructions,* the Reverend Henry McNeal Turner, a Georgia state senator expelled from office in 1868, protested that "Congress, after aiding Mr. Lincoln to take me out of servile slavery, did not intend to put me and my race in *political* slavery" (6).

58. While southern elites used race to trump class concerns and establish the loyalty of poor and middle-class whites, they simultaneously argued to northern audiences that much of the mob violence in their region was at the hands of poor whites, whom they could best control.

Stephen Kantrowitz, "One Man's Mob Is Another Man's Militia: Violence, Manhood, and Authority in Reconstruction South Carolina," in *Jumpin' Jim Crow: Southern Politics from Civil War to Civil Rights*, ed. Jane Dailey, Glenda Elizabeth Gilmore, and Bryant Simon (Princeton, NJ: Princeton University Press, 2000).

59. Cox Richardson, *Death of Reconstruction*, 203.

60. Richard B. Russell, "Declaration of Constitutional Principles," March 12, 1956, *Congressional Record*, 84th Cong., 2nd sess., 4460–61, http://congressional.proquest.com/congressional/docview/t19.d20.cr -1956-0312?accountid=15054. This Declaration was more commonly called the Southern Manifesto. See also Fite, *Richard B. Russell, Jr.*

61. Williamson, *Crucible of Race*, 249–55.

62. Williamson, *Crucible of Race*, 209–10.

63. This trend continues into the current era, with southern states having the preponderance of race-neutral voter identification laws, the onus of which falls disproportionately on minorities and which at least one Democratic Party official (former DNC Chairwoman Debbie Wasserman Schultz) has likened to modern-day Jim Crow. See Ben Smith, "DWS: GOP Wants to Bring Back 'Jim Crow,'" *Politico*, June 6, 2011, http://www.politico.com/blogs/ben-smith/2011/06/dws-gop-wants-to -bring-back-jim-crow-036413.

64. Richard Henry Dana, "Grasp of War," in Michael Les Benedict, *The Fruits of Victory: Alternatives in Restoring the Union, 1865–1877* (Philadelphia: Lippincott, 1975), part 2, document 7.

65. Foner, *Politics and Ideology*, 127.

66. Skowronek, "The Reassociation of Ideas and Purposes," 391–94.

67. Skowronek ("The Reassociation of Ideas and Purposes") makes clear the relation of Wilson to Johnson, both in their shared ideas (and the southern racism at work in these ideas) and, in moments, in their demagogic behaviors.

CHAPTER FOUR

1. Rick Perlstein, *Before the Storm: Barry Goldwater and the Unmaking of the American Consensus* (New York: Hill and Wang, 2001), x–xi.

2. The most well-known complaint about the midcentury American party system came in the American Political Science Association (APSA), "Toward a More Responsible Two-Party System: A Report of the Committee on Political Parties of the American Political Science Association," *American Political Science Review* 44, no. 3, pt. 2 (1950):

1–99. For supporters as well as critics of the American system, this became the standard characterization of the two parties until the 1990s.

3. Quoted in Alan Brinkley, "The Problem of American Conservatism," *American Historical Review* 99, no. 2 (April 1994): 411.

4. Nixon and Buchanan quotes in Steven Hayward, "Extremism and Moderation," *Claremont Review of Books* 14, no. 3 (Summer 2014): 17.

5. Perlstein, *Before the Storm*, 513.

6. Jeff Jacoby, "Liberals Now Love Barry Goldwater but His 1964 Loss Won the GOP's Future," *Boston Globe*, April 20, 2014, https://www.bostonglobe.com/opinion/editorials/2014/04/19/goldwater-lost-landslide-but-made-conservative-politics-mainstream/5O0DYjoRD3GS0ENca2rKvN/story.html.

7. George F. Will, "'The Cheerful Malcontent,'" *Washington Post*, May 31, 1998, C7.

8. For the classic "fringe" statement, see Richard Hofstadter, *The Paranoid Style in American Politics and Other Essays* (New York: Alfred A. Knopf, 1965). For a review of the evolution of the literature, see Julian E. Zelizer, "Rethinking the History of American Conservatism," *Reviews in American History* 38 (2010): 367–92.

9. There was resonance for this in popular culture in the wake of Reagan's victory. A 1981 satiric poster achieved commercial success for the two Harvard business students who created it by playing on the movie title *Bedtime for Bonzo*, retitling it *Bedtime for Brezhnev*. On the poster, credit for the original concept is given to Barry Goldwater. Retrieved on December 12, 2016, from the Kentucky Historical Society, http://kyhistory.pastperfectonline.com/webobject/D9ECBC0D-7EC6-4516-A3F7-41923915147.

10. Donald T. Critchlow, *The Conservative Ascendancy: How the GOP Right Made Political History* (Cambridge, MA: Harvard University Press, 2007), 43.

11. Critchlow, *The Conservative Ascendancy*, 67.

12. APSA, *Toward a More Responsible Party System*.

13. Compare, for example, Barry Goldwater, *Conscience of a Conservative* (Shepherdsville, KY: Victor, 1960); John F. Kennedy, *Profiles in Courage* (New York: Harper and Brothers, 1956); Bill Clinton, *The Man from Hope: With a Special Personal Message from Bill Clinton*, directed by Jeffrey Tuchman (campaign video produced for the 1992 Democratic National Convention, 1992), Barack Obama, *Dreams from My Father: A Story of Race and Inheritance* (New York: Three Rivers Press, 2004),

and Obama, *The Audacity of Hope: Thoughts on Reclaiming the American Dream* (New York: Three Rivers Press, 2006); or Ronald Reagan with Richard Gibson Hubler *Where's the Rest of Me?* (New York: Duell, Sloan and Pearce, 1965).

14. Hayward, "Extremism and Moderation," 19.

15. It wasn't just FDR who eschewed the label of philosophy for his efforts. In *The Liberal Tradition in America* (New York: Harcourt, Brace, 1955), Louis Hartz referred to FDR's policy pursuits as the result of "non-philosophic pragmatism."

16. Goldwater supported the Social Security program as benefits were the result of individual effort but counseled that it should be supplementary to voluntary programs.

17. Goldwater repeatedly argued that desegregation was good public policy. However, he believed that it should be state and local policy, not the product of national intervention. For an interview with Goldwater about his stance on race and civil rights just prior to the 1964 campaign, see Stewart Alsop, "Can Goldwater Win in 64?" *Saturday Evening Post*, August 24, 1963, 19–25, http://www.saturdayeveningpost .com/wp-content/uploads/satevepost/1963-08-24.pdf.

18. Based on his interview with Charles Lichenstein. Critchlow, *The Conservative Ascendancy*, 75 and n. 306.

19. Quoted in Hayward, "Extremism and Moderation," 21. In the original ("The Goldwater Myth"), written in 2009, Frum argues that Goldwater was an unmitigated disaster for Republicans and that Reagan's subsequent success owes more to Carter's failures, and that of the Democrats more generally, than anything that Goldwater may have given him. Frum does this to caution Republicans against embracing a strategy of nominating extremists and failing to modernize their message. Our claim is that Democratic policies of the 1960s and 1970s were perceived to be failures by an electorate that Goldwater had primed to see them that way. See David Frum, "The Goldwater Myth," in "The Meaning of the Goldwater Campaign" (AEI forum publication, March 2, 2009), http://www.aei.org/publication/the-meaning-of-the -goldwater-campaign/.

20. Quoted in Robert D. McFadden, "Harry V. Jaffa, Conservative Scholar and Goldwater Muse, Dies at 96," *New York Times*, January 12, 2015, http://www.nytimes.com/2015/01/12/us/politics/harry-v -jaffa-conservative-scholar-and-goldwater-muse-dies-at-96.html.

21. See Stephen Skowronek, *The Politics Presidents Make: Leadership from John Adams to Bill Clinton*, 2nd ed., rev. (Cambridge, MA: Belknap Press, 1998).

22. See William A. Rusher, *The Rise of the Right* (New York: William Morrow, 1984). On factional dynamics, also see Howard L. Reiter and Jeffrey M. Stonecash, *Counter-Realignment: Political Change in the Northeastern United States* (New York: Cambridge University Press, 2011); Nicol C. Rae, *The Decline and Fall of the Liberal Republicans: From 1952 to the Present* (New York: Oxford University Press, 1989).

23. For examples, see Rick Perlstein, *Before the Storm*; Kim Phillips-Fein, *Invisible Hands: The Making of the Conservative Movement from the New Deal to Reagan* (New York: Norton, 2009); Jeffrey Hart, *The Making of the American Conservative Mind: National Review and Its Times* (Wilmington, DE: ISI Books, 2005); Alice O'Connor "Financing the Counter Revolution," in *Rightward Bound: Making America Conservative in the 1970s*, ed. Bruce J. Schulman and Julian E. Zelizer (Cambridge, MA: Harvard University Press, 2008); Jonathan M. Schoenwald, *A Time for Choosing: The Rise of Modern American Conservatism* (New York: Oxford University Press, 2001).

24. Hart, *The Making of the American Conservative Mind*, 141–46.

25. In Lee Edwards, "Barry M. Goldwater: The Most Consequential Loser in American Politics," Heritage Foundation's Makers of American Political Thought Series, no. 11, July 3, 2014, http://www .heritage.org/research/reports/2014/07/barry-m-goldwater-the-most -consequential-loser-in-american-politics.

26. Historian Steven Hayward notes that Goldwater received over 1 million donations to his campaign, whereas Nixon received just 40,000 contributions four years prior. See Jeff Jacoby, "Liberals now Love Barry Goldwater." Seventy-two percent of contributions to the Goldwater campaign were sums under $500, many solicited through direct mail campaigns. See Mary C. Brennan, "Winning the War/Losing the Battle: The Goldwater Presidential Campaign and Its Effects on the Evolution of Modern Conservatism," in *The Conservative Sixties*, ed. David Farber and Jeff Roche (New York: Peter Lang, 2003), 71.

27. For a terrific account of the creative marketing steps taken by Manion and others, see Perlstein, *Before the Storm*, 61–68.

28. Critchlow, *The Conservative Ascendancy*, 41–76.

29. Hayward, "Extremism and Moderation," 19. As Hayward points

out, Goldwater's ideas were also directly and widely disseminated through a twice-weekly newspaper column he wrote, ghostwritten by Steven Shadegg, that was syndicated by the *Los Angeles Times* and appeared in more than 150 newspapers.

30. Rusher, *The Rise of the Right*, 164–65, and Hart, *The Making of the American Conservative Mind*, 149.

31. Rowland Evans and Robert Novak, "Goldwater Still Hasn't Made His Decision," *St. Petersburg Times*, December 20, 1963, 10-A.

32. Quoted in Robert Alan Goldberg, *Barry Goldwater* (New Haven, CT: Yale University Press, 1995), 143.

33. Evans and Novak, "Goldwater Still Hasn't Made His Decision."

34. Barry M. Goldwater with Jack Casserly, *Goldwater* (New York: Doubleday, 1988), 153–54.

35. Goldberg, *Barry Goldwater*, chap. 8. Also see Perlstein, *Before the Storm*, 371–405, quotes on 382–83.

36. Quotes in Perlstein, *Before the Storm*, 382–83.

37. John B. Judis, "Barry Goldwater's Curious Campaign," *Alicia Patterson Foundation Reporter* 8, no. 4 (1985), http://www.aliciapatterson .org/stories/barry-goldwaters-curious-campaign.

38. Many observers have noted the disproportionate organizational success of the contemporary Tea Party movement, which has combined top-down fund-raising and resources with bottom-up organization and mobilization, in some ways reminiscent of the Goldwater campaign. Indeed, in their study of the Tea Party, Theda Skocpol and Vanessa Williamson found that many grassroots members fondly recalled the Goldwater campaign as their introduction to, and training ground for, conservative politics. See Theda Skocpol and Vanessa Williamson, *The Tea Party and the Remaking of Republican Conservatism* (New York: Oxford University Press, 2013).

39. Hart, *The Making of the American Conservative Mind*, 141–42. Also see Nixon's 1960 nomination acceptance speech at the Republican National Convention, http://www.presidency.ucsb.edu/ws/index.php ?pid=25974.

40. Rusher, *The Rise of the Right*, 195. Nixon felt the wrath of conservatives at the 1960 convention, after his "Treaty of Fifth Avenue" with Nelson Rockefeller. As one Nixon operative explained about conservative anger at the convention, to win "we called in every political IOU we held in the country that night." See Goldberg, *Barry Goldwater*,

145. He learned the value of conservatives again in 1962, after a tough primary fight in the California gubernatorial race. But the conservative movement's national power was driven home for him at the 1964 Republican convention.

41. Republicans as early as the 1950s had sensed the compatibility of their party's emphasis on limited government with the white South's emphasis on states' rights, and Eisenhower, who sought to build the party's infrastructure in the region, won several states in the South in 1952 and 1956. See Nicole Mellow, *The State of Disunion: Regional Sources of Modern American Partisanship* (Baltimore, MD: Johns Hopkins University Press, 2008), 51; and on Eisenhower, see Daniel J. Galvin, *Presidential Party Building: Dwight D. Eisenhower to George W. Bush* (Princeton, NJ: Princeton University Press, 2010). A more explicit and concerted effort, however, didn't emerge until Nixon's presidency. Some authors emphasize the ways in which Nixon (along with George Wallace) took advantage of southern white backlash; others emphasize a broader set of economic, industrial, and demographic changes. See, for example, Dan T. Carter, *From George Wallace to Newt Gingrich: Race in the Conservative Counterrevolution, 1963–1994* (Baton Rouge: Louisiana State University Press, 2000); Matthew D. Lassiter, *The Silent Majority: Suburban Politics in the Sunbelt South* (Princeton, NJ: Princeton University Press, 2007); Earl Black and Merle Black, *The Vital South: How Presidents Are Elected* (Cambridge, MA: Harvard University Press, 1992); Thomas Byrne Edsall and Mary D. Edsall, *Chain Reaction: The Impact of Race, Rights, and Taxes on American Politics* (New York: Norton, 1992); Joseph Crespino, *In Search of Another Country: Mississippi and the Conservative Counterrevolution* (Princeton, NJ: Princeton University Press, 2009); and Mellow, *State of Disunion*.

42. Quoted in Garry Wills, *Nixon Agonistes: The Crisis of the Self-Made Man* (Boston: Houghton Mifflin, 2002), 265.

43. Judis, "Barry Goldwater's Curious Campaign." Also see Goldberg, *Barry Goldwater*, on the role of Goldwater's western identity in shaping his political philosophy.

44. "Gut conservative" is how journalist and secret campaign adviser Ralph De Toledano described Goldwater. Judis, "Barry Goldwater's Curious Campaign."

45. As Goldberg has written in *Barry Goldwater*, about the West in particular: "The emergence of the West as a key factor in the political

equation enhanced Goldwater's credibility. Without a western brand, would Barry Goldwater have stirred as much enthusiasm? Would his rise have been so swift if the region was stagnant and unable to claim its reputation as the land of the boom and the second chance?" (134).

46. Goldwater's anticommunist rhetoric was peppered with language suggestive of frontier masculinity. For example, he privately criticized Kennedy's "gutless character" during the Bay of Pigs invasion, especially in comparison to his "toughness of mind and will to lead the country." John W. Dean and Barry M. Goldwater Jr., *Pure Goldwater* (New York: Palgrave Macmillan, 2008), 118; Lee Edwards, *Goldwater: The Man Who Made a Revolution* (Washington, DC: Regnery, 1995), 174–75.

47. Critchlow, *The Conservative Ascendancy*, 56–59; Goldberg, *Barry Goldwater*, 137–38.

48. See Goldberg, *Barry Goldwater*. To be clear, Goldwater was nevertheless loyal to the Republican Party and is perhaps best understood, then, as a member of the loyal opposition. See Rusher, *The Rise of the Right*, 155: "At heart Goldwater was, and remains, a perfectly orthodox, budget-balancing, main-line Republican, whose heart beats in near perfect accord with Jerry Ford's."

49. Alsop, "Can Goldwater Win in 64?" 23. Alsop also points out that Goldwater benefited from the "new money" in the South and the West: "Wherever there is a lot of new money in the United States—in the West and Southwest, in Texas, in the newly industrialized South—there is fanatical Goldwater support."

50. "Senator Goldwater Speaks Out on the Issues," Political Tract issued by Goldwater for President Committee (1964), 16.

51. Larry J. Sabato, "How Goldwater Changed Campaigns Forever," *Politico*, October 27, 2014, 3.

52. Edwards, *Goldwater: The Man Who Made a Revolution*, 360.

53. J. William Middendorf II, *A Glorious Disaster: Barry Goldwater's Presidential Campaign and the Origins of the Conservative Movement* (New York: Basic Books, 2006), chap. 20.

54. Rusher, *The Rise of the Right*, 195.

55. The states that didn't go for Nixon in 1968 were concentrated in the Northeast (with the exceptions of New Hampshire, Vermont, and New Jersey), and the four states of the Deep South (Georgia, Alabama, Mississippi, and Louisiana), which voted for George Wallace instead.

56. Goldberg, *Barry Goldwater*, 154.

57. Goldberg, *Barry Goldwater*, 89.

58. Though he accepted the constitutionality of the desegregation of passenger rails and terminals. Goldberg, *Barry Goldwater*, 154.

59. Goldwater's famous admonition that Republicans should "go hunting where the ducks are," delivered to an Atlanta audience in 1961, is often treated as the beginning of the Republican southern strategy, one focused exclusively on appealing to southern whites upset about civil rights for African Americans. In actuality, the statement was intended as a rebuke to Nixon and Rockefeller for their efforts to actively woo African Americans by pledging aggressive national action on civil rights (with which Goldwater did not agree). It is not clear, however, and is in fact unlikely, that Goldwater intended the statement as it's been interpreted—an invitation to the Republican Party to engage in race baiting to capture the South. What is more consistent with Goldwater's leadership and campaign overall is that he was suggesting Republicans pursue white Southerners (and Westerners) on their many grounds of compatibility, including the principle of states' rights. See the remarks of key Goldwater operative, J. William Middendorf II, *A Glorious Disaster*, 109–10. Also Perlstein, *Before the Storm*, 364. Also see Alsop's discussion of Goldwater, race, and civil rights in "Can Goldwater Win in 64?"

60. Goldberg, *Barry Goldwater*, 154.

61. In this context, it is interesting to compare Goldwater's consistency on principles and his related, nuanced response to civil rights with the unprincipled flip-flopping and political expediency with which LBJ approached the issue of civil rights. The president is typically recalled as the hero who campaigned for, and signed into law, the 1964 Act while declaring "We Shall Overcome" to Congress; yet up until 1964, including his time as Senate Majority Leader, he consistently voted against civil rights legislation.

62. Goldberg, *Barry Goldwater*, 251.

63. Rick Perlstein, *Nixonland: The Rise of a President and the Fracturing of America* (New York: Scribner, 2008), 88.

64. Perlstein, *Nixonland*, 89.

65. Perlstein, *Nixonland*, 88.

66. See, for example, Bruce H. Kalk, "Wormley's Hotel Revisited: Richard Nixon's Southern Strategy and the End of the Second Reconstruction," *North Carolina Historical Review* 71, no. 1 (January 1994):

88; Dewey Grantham, *The Life and Death of the Solid South: A Political History* (Lexington: University Press of Kentucky, 1992), 178, and Wills, *Nixon Agonistes*, 251–57.

67. For arguments about the suburban strategy that extend beyond race, see Matthew Lassiter, *The Silent Majority: Suburban Politics in the Sunbelt South* (Princeton, NJ: Princeton University Press, 2007); Edsall and Edsall, *Chain Reaction*; Mellow, *The State of Disunion*; Lisa McGirr, *Suburban Warriors: The Origins of the New American Right* (Princeton, NJ: Princeton University Press, 2002); and Bruce J. Shulman, *From Cotton Belt to Sun Belt: Federal Policy, Economic Development, and the Transformation of the South 1938–1980* (Durham, NC: Duke University Press, 1994). McGirr's book (*Suburban Warrior*), in particular, focuses on suburban conservatism in the West and places a greater emphasis on social conservatism.

68. For a particularly thoughtful description of how the explicitly race-based politics of the Jim Crow South was transformed into a broader conservative suburban politics where race was an implicit undertone, see Kevin Kruse, *White Flight: Atlanta and the Making of Modern Conservatism* (Princeton, NJ: Princeton University Press, 2010).

69. See Perlstein, *Before the Storm*, 138. Also, Goldberg, *Barry Goldwater*, 253.

70. Dean and Goldwater, *Pure Goldwater*, 347, 353, 369. Also Goldberg, *Barry Goldwater*.

71. Critchlow, *The Conservative Ascendancy*, 77–103; Rusher, *The Rise of the Right*, 179–208.

72. Robert Mason, *Richard Nixon and the Quest for a New Majority* (Chapel Hill: University of North Carolina Press, 2004), 6.

73. Critchlow, *The Conservative Ascendancy*, 93.

74. Mark Bowden, *Guests of the Ayatollah: The First Battle in America's War with Militant Islam* (New York: Atlantic Monthly Press, 2006), 243, 378.

75. See Peter Schweizer, *Reagan's War: The Epic Story of His Forty-Year Struggle and Final Triumph over Communism* (New York: Doubleday, 2002); and Jay Winik, *On the Brink: The Dramatic, Behind-the Scenes Sagas of the Reagan Era and the Men and Women Who Won the Cold War* (New York: Simon and Schuster, 1996). In criticizing Carter's handling of the crisis, Reagan sounded much like Goldwater had when he criticized President Kennedy for being soft on Cuba and in Vietnam. See,

for example, Dean and Goldwater, *Pure Goldwater*, 132–35. Also, Edwards, *Goldwater: The Man Who Made a Revolution*, 174–76.

76. Joseph McCartin, "Turnabout Years: Public Sector Unionism and the Fiscal Crisis," in *Rightward Bound*, ed. Bruce J. Shulman and Julian E. Zelizer (Cambridge, MA: Harvard University Press, 2008), 210–26.

77. Social conservatism was also a major component of the Reagan campaign, but not an effective one until at least 1994, by which time it also clearly represented a distortion of Goldwater's positions. Goldwater himself was highly critical of this element of the Republican resurgence.

78. Perlstein, *Before the Storm*, 333.

79. Sabato, "How Goldwater Changed Campaigns Forever."

80. Jacoby, "Liberals now Love Barry Goldwater, but His 1964 Loss Won the GOP's Future." Alsop also discusses Goldwater's essential likability in "Can Goldwater Win in 64?"

81. The quote is widely attributed to a reporter at the convention who said it in apparent amazement to writer Theodore White. See Mary Brennan, *Turning Right in the Sixties: The Conservative Capture of the GOP* (Chapel Hill: University of North Carolina Press, 1995), 78.

82. Sabato, "How Goldwater Changed Campaigns Forever."

83. As vice chair of the Phoenix city council in 1949, he was the highest Republican officeholder in the state. He quickly parlayed that experience and his contacts, into managing the campaign of another Republican who won the vacant seat for governor of Arizona and then two years later won his own campaign for the Senate unseating a popular Democratic incumbent. Perlstein, *Before the Storm*, 21–22.

84. Perlstein, *Before the Storm*, 18.

85. Hayward, "Extremism and Moderation," 17. Also, McFadden, "Harry V. Jaffa, Conservative Scholar and Goldwater Muse, Dies at 96." As Hayward writes (21), figures in the media, such as *Washington Post* reporter David Broder, acknowledged after the campaign that they presented an unfair picture of Goldwater, obscuring his "essential decency." And as Goldwater himself remarked, in true Goldwater fashion, "If I had to go by the media reports alone, I'd have voted against the sonofabitch, too."

86. Farber and Roche, *The Conservative Sixties*.

87. George F. Will, "Cruz Is Aiming at the Wrong Republicans," *Washington Post*, April 1, 2015.

88. George F. Will, "'The Cheerful Malcontent.'"

89. Paul Ryan, "Americans Deserve a Choice," speech delivered at CPAC, Washington, DC, February 9, 2012, retrieved at *National Review* Online, http://www.nationalreview.com/corner/290721/text-paul -ryans-cpac-speech-nr-staff. Goldwater was adamant in his repudiation of social conservatism. Of the religious right, he said, "Do not associate my name with anything you do—you're extremists, and you've hurt the Republican Party much more than the Democrats have." Quoted in Gregg Segal, "I Was a Teenage Conservative," *American Prospect*, December 5, 2012.

CHAPTER FIVE

1. Meredith Shiner, "Can Ted Cruz Go from Obstructionist in Chief to Commander in Chief?" *Yahoo News*, March 22, 2015, http:// news.yahoo.com/can-ted-cruz-go-from-obstructionist-in-chief-to -commander-in-chief-212751655.html.

2. Partisan integrity, as we describe it here, is very similar to Russell Muirhead's idea of "better partisanship." Russell Muirhead, *The Promise of Party in a Polarized Era* (Cambridge, MA: Harvard University Press, 2014). Goldwater was not a demagogue. However, he certainly suffered from the demagoguery of his opponents, as is well illustrated by the famous "daisy" television commercial depicting the cost of a Goldwater victory to be a mushroom cloud.

3. See, for example, the debate between Bruce Miroff ("Leadership and American Political Development," ch. 3) and Adam Sheingate ("The Terrain of the Political Entrepreneur," ch. 2) in *Formative Acts: American Politics in the Making*, ed. Steven Skowronek and Matthew Glassman (Philadelphia: University of Pennsylvania Press, 2007). See also Jeffrey K. Tulis, "The Possibility of Constitutional Statesmanship," in *The Limits of Constitutional Democracy*, ed. Jeffrey K. Tulis and Stephen Macedo (Princeton, NJ: Princeton University Press, 2010).

4. According to William Riker, rational choice theory would predict that both sides would "go negative." While Riker greatly overstates his case in general, his assumption proves to be truer of the most articulate Anti-Federalists than of *The Federalist*. Indeed, as we discuss in chapter 2, *The Federalist* devotes considerable effort to mollifying the uncertain citizen rather than attacking the writers' opponents. In the very first number, *The Federalist* appeals to reason over passion and opines

that there are "wise and good men on the wrong as well as the right side of questions of the first magnitude for society. This circumstance, if duly attended to, would furnish a lesson of moderation to those who are ever so thoroughly persuaded of being in the right in any controversy." William H. Riker, "Why Negative Campaigning Is Rational: The Rhetoric of the Ratification Campaign of 1787–1788," *Studies in American Political Development* 5, no. 2 (October 1991). For a critique of Riker's theory, see Jeffrey K. Tulis, "Riker's Rhetoric of Ratification" in the same issue, along with Riker's response to Tulis.

5. William G. Howell and Terry M. Moe, *Relic: How Our Constitution Undermines Effective Government and Why We Need a More Powerful Presidency* (New York: Basic Books, 2016).

6. Theodore J. Lowi, *The Personal President: Power Invested, Promise Unfulfilled* (Ithaca, NY: Cornell University Press, 1985), 24.

7. Lowi, *Personal President*, 46.

8. Similar arguments have been made about Reconstruction and are vulnerable to the same criticism. See Paul E. Peterson, *The Price of Federalism* (Washington, DC: Brookings Institution Press, 1995).

9. One scholar who has a similar understanding of the subtle relationship between the political logic of the Constitution and Progressivism is Daniel Carpenter, "Completing the Constitution: Progressive-Era Economic Regulation and the Political Perfection of Article I, Section 8," in Stephen Skowronek, Stephen M. Engel, and Bruce Ackerman, eds., *The Progressives Century: Political Reform, Constitutional Government, and the Modern American State* (New Haven, CT: Yale University Press, 2016), ch. 13.

10. See Herbert J. Storing, "The Problem of Big Government," and "The Role of Government in Society," in *Toward a More Perfect Union*, ed. Joseph M. Bessette (Washington, DC: AEI Press, 1995).

11. Ackerman cogently describes the ways that he is indebted to Hartz and the ways in which he disagrees with him. Bruce Ackerman, *We the People*, vol. 1, *Foundations* (Cambridge, MA: Belknap Press, 1991), 25–29.

12. Stephen Skowronek, "The Reassociation of Ideas and Purposes: Racism, Liberalism, and the American Political Tradition," *American Political Science Review* 100, no. 3 (August 2006): 385.

13. The idea that transformative change does not thoroughly dislodge the prior policies and practices it aims to repudiate has an established

lineage in American political development scholarship. Foundational studies, such as Karen Orren *Belated Feudalism: Labor, the Law, and Liberal Development in the United States* (New York: Cambridge University Press, 1992), highlight this, and Stephen Skowronek and Karen Orren, in *The Search for American Political Development* (New York: Cambridge University Press, 2004), identify this feature of American political life as an animating concern of current research.

14. Smith shows that illiberal practices have always been far more extensive and deeply institutionalized than most scholars have seen or acknowledged. He shows how the sustenance of liberalism itself, a project he endorses, requires better understanding of and confrontation with the ascriptive tradition. Although Smith identifies three traditions, he devotes most of his attention to two, liberalism and ascriptive hierarchies. See Rogers Smith, "Beyond Tocqueville, Myrdal, and Hartz: The Multiple Traditions in America," *American Political Science Review* 87, no. 3 (September 1983); also his *Civic Ideals: Conflicting Visions of Citizenship in U.S. History* (New Haven, CT: Yale University Press, 1999).

15. Skowronek, "The Reassociation of Ideas and Purposes."

16. Michael Rogin, *Ronald Reagan the Movie: And Other Episodes in Political Demonology* (Berkeley: University of California Press, 1988).

17. Uday Singh Mehta, "Liberal Strategies of Exclusion," *Politics and Society* 18, no. 4 (1990): 427–54. Also see his *Liberalism and Empire: A Study in Nineteenth Century British Liberal Thought* (Chicago: University of Chicago Press, 1999). Brian Danhoff applies Mehta's argument to the United States. See Danhoff, "'They Are Children and We Are Men': 'Civilizational Infantilism' and American Political Thought," *New England Journal of Political Science* 7, no. 2 (Fall 2013): 236–71.

18. Smith, "Beyond Tocqueville, Myrdal, and Hartz," 558–59.

19. Smith, "Beyond Tocqueville, Myrdal, and Hartz," 558.

20. See Robert A. Goldwin, *From Parchment to Power: How James Madison Used the Bill of Rights to Save the Constitution* (Washington, DC: AEI Press, 1997); Herbert Storing, "The Constitution and the Bill of Rights," in *Toward a More Perfect Union: Writings of Herbert J. Storing*, ed. Joseph M. Bessette (Washington, DC: AEI Press, 1995); Michael J. Klarman, *The Framers' Coup: The Making of the United States Constitution* (New York: Oxford University Press, 2016), chap. 7; Richard Labunski, *James Madison and the Struggle for the Bill of Rights* (New York: Oxford University Press, 2006).

21. The same jurists most likely to ignore Hamilton's warning, now inscribed in the Ninth and Tenth Amendments about the constitutional interpretation of rights, by denying that there are implied rights are among those who heartedly endorse the idea that there are implied powers. See Stephen Macedo, *The New Right v. The Constitution* (Washington, DC: Cato Institute, 1987).

22. Mary Ann Glendon, *Rights Talk: The Impoverishment of Political Discourse* (New York: Free Press, 1991).

23. See Herbert Storing, "Federalists and Anti-Federalists: The Ratification Debate," in *Toward a More Perfect Union: Writings of Herbert J. Storing*, ed. Joseph M. Bessette (Washington, DC: AEI Press, 1995), 39n7.

24. For a very different but not inconsistent understanding, see Andreas Kalyvas and Ira Katznelson, *Liberal Beginnings: Making a Republic for the Moderns* (New York: Cambridge University Press, 2008).

25. Frederick Douglass, "Address for the Promotion of Colored Enlistments" July 6, 1863 in *The Life and Writings of Frederick Douglass*, ed. Phillip S. Foner (New York: International Publishers, 1975), 3:365, cited in Herbert J. Storing, "Slavery and the Moral Foundations of the Republic," in *The Moral Foundations of the American Republic*, 3rd ed., ed. Robert H. Horwitz (Charlottesville: University Press of Virginia, 1986), 320.

26. "Remarks by the President at the Memorial Service for Fallen Police Officers," Dallas, TX, July 12, 2016, White House, Office of the Press Secretary, https://www.whitehouse.gov/the-press-office/2016/07/12/remarks-president-memorial-service-fallen-dallas-police-officers.

Index